One Thousand
ELSEWHERE
A True Survivor Story

Keeya Vawar

Publisher's Cataloging-in-Publication data

Names: Vawar, Keeya, author. Roberts, Christine, editor. Greene III, Robert, cover design.
Title: One Thousand Elsewhere: A True Survivor Story / Keeya Vawar.
Description: Hurst, TX: First Fruits Publishing, 2022.
Identifiers: LCCN: 2021951170 | ISBN: 978-1-7363340-0-3 (hardcover) | 978-1-7363340-1-0 (paperback) | 978-1-7363340-2-7 (ebook) | 978-1-7363340-3-4 (audio)
Subjects: LCSH Vawar, Keeya. | Child trafficking victims--Biography. | Human trafficking victims--Biography. | Runaway children--Biography. | African Americans--Biography. | Women--Biography. | Dysfunctional families--Biography. | BISAC BIOGRAPHY & AUTOBIOGRAPHY / Personal Memoirs | BIOGRAPHY & AUTOBIOGRAPHY / Women | BIOGRAPHY & AUTOBIOGRAPHY / Cultural, Ethnic & Regional / African American & Black | BIOGRAPHY & AUTOBIOGRAPHY / Survival | BIOGRAPHY & AUTOBIOGRAPHY / Religious
Classification: LCC 362.760973. V39 2022 | DDC 362.76/092--dc23 | Copywrite © 2022 | Printed in the United States of America

ALL RIGHTS RESERVED. No part of this book may be reproduced in any form without permission in writing from the publisher, except in the case of brief quotations embodied in critical reviews or articles. www.keeyavawar.com

To all of the people trapped in human trafficking or any other situation that took advantage of your innocence through abuse—may you see freedom and healing from God. May He wipe your tears away and give you a new story! You are valuable!

Acknowledgements

To my earthly parents, Nezzie Shabazz and Robert M. A. Greene Jr., who God used to send me to Earth. Mommy—thanks for teaching me how to forgive. It was the greatest lesson I learned. Thanks for always being available to listen to my heart and for giving us the best that you knew how to give through it all. Thank you for showing me that when I mess things up, I can admit the wrongs and do what I can to make things right. Daddy—thank you for making sure we went to church. We may have never developed relationships with God otherwise. You are forgiven!

To my brother, Tony—you were my protector and first friend in this life. I have always believed that you are a genius. The most wonderful childhood memories I have were when we entertained each other or fell deeply into mischief and adventure. The stories you made up when I was little and the ways in which we coped with our lives became the hope I needed during some of my darkest days. Making you proud of me has been a goal of mine for as long as I can remember.

To my husband, John—thank you for being a man who was not afraid of my story but has been brave enough to walk by my side. You have endured my reality, you have wiped away my tears as God healed my aching heart, you have challenged me in ways that are for my good, and you have made me laugh. Thank you for all that you continue to do!

To my children, John III, Ajeanai, and Christian—you know me best! I'm grateful to God for each of your lives. You all are my gifts! Thank you for returning all the love I could muster up and pour into you. You have spoken life and love into me at critical times. You are a joy, and I am blessed that you love me! God has so much in store for your lives. Thank you for accepting all of my unconventional methods in order that you might turn out to be decent, God-fearing people despite being raised by your imperfect parents.

To all of the people who were a part of my journey who did something to hurt me knowingly or unknowingly—I forgive you and pray that if you don't know Him, you will meet Jesus and allow Him to transform your lives!

To all of my friends and extended family, who love me even though you may not understand me at times—thank you for being a part of my life! To all of my mentors, thank you for seeing in me what I could not and for adding such value to my life! Thank you for giving me all of the love that you know how to give and thank you for the prayers and laughs! Thank you to the beautiful young lady in the youth group, who told me that my name stood for *Keep Encouraging Everyone Young Adult*. I will endeavor to do that through the power of Christ Jesus who lives in me!'

To Neil Foote and Richelle Payne for being the best PR team in the world—thank you for putting up with me and guiding me through the process with care and professionalism.

And, lastly, to Christine Roberts, my ride-or-die editor, who went over and above to ensure the integrity of the product—thank you!

Disclaimer

This book is a nonfiction account of my teenage and young adult years. I've divulged intimate details that would be considered sensitive content not for pity but for a point of reference. My prayer is that you understand that my mission is to uplift, encourage and give you hope no matter your situation, or what you personally escaped. So hang on to your seat, and read until the end!

Contents

Dedication 3
Acknowledgements 4
Disclaimer 7
Foreword 9
Preface: The Fruit of My Family's Tree 15
Chapter 1: The Fight 22
Chapter 2: Tulsa 30
Chapter 3: Life Happens to Us All 49
Chapter 4: Leaving Dallas 65
Chapter 5: My Ticket to Freedom? 73
Chapter 6: The Shock 83
Chapter 7: In Too Deep 102
Chapter 8: Under the Radar 115
Chapter 9: On the Run 130
Chapter 10: The Masquerade 141
Chapter 11: Absconded 151
Chapter 12: Attempting Normalcy 163
Chapter 13: At All Costs 170
Chapter 14: The Wire 179
Chapter 15: Jagged-Edged Emotions 190
Chapter 16: Like a Moth to a Flame 204
Chapter 17: How Do You Want It? 223
Chapter 18: Back to Life! 247

Foreword

"We have a little sister, and her breasts are not yet grown. What shall we do for our sister on the day she is spoken for? If she is a wall, we will build a tower of silver to protect her. If she is a door, we will enclose her with panels of cedar."
– Song of Solomon 8:8-9

It had to have been about 20 years ago when I watched this timid, eager young woman take her seat in a meeting with me. She was reporting to work as an intern at an ad agency where I worked. We were the industry leader for producing the donuts (or the opening and closing sequences) and negotiating the airtime for ministries that broadcast weekly TV programs.

I had just relocated to Dallas after having served as chief spokesperson for an HBCU in the Southeast. I left even though I was performing at the top of my game because my job nearly suffocated my spirit. I chose the path less traveled. I chose to honor my soul rather than give in to the pressure to go farther and faster in my career. In hindsight, it seems I needed to meet Keeya Vawar as much as she needed to learn anything from me.

The agency recruited me to establish their first-ever public relations practice area. It would be a value-added service to the ministries that worked with us but I was also responsible for sustainability. The business of buying and selling air time during the religious block on TV was a relatively new phenomenon in the late 90s. I was one-third of the agency's Dream Team that traveled across North America to pitch and close business. We set up an internship program with The Potter's House of Dallas and Keeya was their top pick. She was pleasant, nervous and full of zest, all of the qualities that I had expected to see in a young, curious new team member.

We got to know each other well as we organized the office doing mundane things. Soon I met her mother and we all celebrated closing deals, birthdays, and other milestones. She asked a lot of questions and I listened to her dreams for the future and sought to provide every opportunity for her to not only learn the fundamentals of public relations and how to build and protect a client's reputation but also see the decisions that went into running an organization for profitability.

She took to it, struggled a bit but never gave less than 100% in effort or intention. She quickly became more of a little sister, someone whose wide doe-eyes suggested to me there was more to her story. For a long time I didn't know her story, her real story. When she hit me with the headlines, I think she thought it would change my opinion of her. It didn't, not one bit. In fact, I shifted into big sister mode but was mindful to give her the space and opportunity to say more, if and when she wanted to tell me more.

Soon after she completed the program, she got married. I moved on, too. We lost touch for a while but I always thought of Keeya every March. I say that with confidence because she and my oldest sister share the same birth date. I said a prayer for her on that day every spring, for years. I think I was hoping the few words I uttered along with her name would somehow blow like winds of refreshing and direction, helping to soothe her along her journey, wherever God was taking her. I believe she is on the other side of it all, and as scripture tells us, she has now turned around to help someone else overcome or avoid what she had endured in her life.

As years passed I wondered if others came alongside her, like the Moabite woman's friends, to be like a wall, showing her how to be firm in character and capacity to withstand the invitations for immorality that would surely come. Or, perhaps she still struggled and was more like an open door with unresolved insecurities and weaknesses. Did she know that each fulfilled different functions: the wall is a defense and the door is for admission? Did she know that life's situations will require her to access different parts of her personality, tap into different skills or show a specific kind of strength? Did she just flee from her captor's location, or was she fully free from their grip?

We know as many as 27 million men, women, and children around the world, including in the United States, are victims of "trafficking in persons," which refers to the act of recruiting, harboring, transporting, providing, or obtaining a person for compelled labor or commercial sex through the use of force, fraud, or coercion. A person younger than 18 who is induced to perform a commercial sex act is considered a trafficking victim regardless of whether any force, fraud, or coercion is used.

According to the U.S. Department of States, "human trafficking can include, but does not require, movement. People may be considered trafficking victims regardless of whether they were born into a state of servitude, were exploited in their hometown, were transported to the exploitative situation, previously consented to work for a trafficker, or participated in a crime as a direct result of being subjected to trafficking."

At the core of this phenomenon is the traffickers' goal of exploiting and enslaving their victims and the myriad coercive and deceptive practices they use to do so.

Our young people will always play critical roles on both sides of the human trafficking spectrum: at one end, they are the most vulnerable to becoming its victims and, at the other, the most qualified to lead its deconstruction. Solutions that will be championed by our young people involve both controlling the wild fire of human trafficking and permanently extinguishing its long-smoldering embers. It is this daring mission upon which we embark with young voices and minds at the forefront, guided by lawmakers and the Church, within the framework of the lessons contained in the pages of this book.

Keeya shares her most painful and perhaps embarrassing memories, and, with tenderness and transparency she shows us how to recognize the warning signs of a victim and that they long to escape their aggressors. With skillful precision she excises the bee's stinger from the flesh because pulling it with force can push even more venom into the body. There is an inexplicable dimension of Keeya's bubbly disposition that empowers her to deliver this emancipation proclamation of sorts with clarity and determination. I can imagine her knees may always quiver with the thought that her story will now be shared outside the walls of her prayer closet, after her husband's embrace, and beyond her closest confidants. But God has written breakthrough into the narrative of her story.

One Thousand Elsewhere is her story. It is her gift to us because if we are honest, we are all trapped in situations, whether or not of our making, from which the escape route is dark, narrow, painful, unpredictable, and foreign. I knew it was time to go. Life called me and will call you to take hold of the more that we know God has in store for us. We must call it in. We must seize the opportunity to escape the grasp of what has held us in captivity.

It's been said that the difference between courage and cowardice is one small step to the side. We must muster the courage to tell our stories. *One Thousand Elsewhere* gives you the blueprint, shows you it's OK and appropriate to not only uncover the shame, but to understand how it attaches itself to you. There's freedom in telling your story, your way. I'm so proud of Keeya for telling her story, without reservation or regret. I applaud her courage and yours, too. If Keeya can wrestle free from the handcuffs of human trafficking then there's hope and help in the pages of this book for us to escape our captivity, too.

Richelle Payne, M.A., CCP

Award-winning Writer, Branding and Business Turnaround Expert, and Communications Coach to the C-suite | Managing Partner, Hurst & Leigh Communications Group LLC | Philadelphia

Contact: richelle@hurstleigh.com or 214-558-0506

The Fruit of My Family's Tree

S et in the 1990s, this book chronicles the hardships and redemption of my teenage years, a life-changing journey that has proven to be quite the journey to write about. But in order for you to know my story, it is important you understand the family I came from.

Let's begin with Daddy, Robert M. A. Greene Jr., who grew up to be a staff sergeant in the United States Air Force.

His mother, Ora Lee Emmons, was well-known around her neighborhood, giving birth to a total of twelve children, who all had different fathers. She was hardened by the street life and showed little skill in nurturing her large brood. Splintered, poor, and broken, the family made do any way they could. The siblings managed to maintain communication whenever possible, but this was difficult because of disagreements between Ora Lee and the various fathers.

As a result, Daddy had extreme abandonment issues growing up. He lived in five foster homes on the South Side of Chicago, Illinois, checkerboarding around low-income neighborhoods and infamous projects in search of love, acceptance, and respect. He never seemed to be able to make a significant connection even with his own father, the late Sergeant Robert M. A. Greene Sr., a Navy man who also served as a Navy cook and as a stand-in for shooting at targets. All I've ever been told about my grandfather is that he was an alcoholic and that he killed one of his sons, a Blackstone Ranger gang member, in self-defense.

Daddy suffered a great deal as a child, and his one ambition seemed to be to break out of the colored realities that haunted and mocked his attempts at success. He was a graduate of Dunbar High School, initially excelling despite his circumstances: his speech was above average because of his love for the English language, his charming personality granted him favor with all kinds of people, and his future seemed promising. He joined the military in hopes of making something of himself, only to be faced with the same street games—but the stakes were much higher. He paid dearly for his involvement in trafficking drugs, which cost him everything, including his Montgomery GI Bill benefits.

With a dishonorable discharge under his belt, a disappointed wife, and two young children, Daddy moved back to the States to start a new life. The regret of poor choices was all he had to his name. His discouragement led him to drink and get deeply involved in intravenous drug use, which, though employed casually in the military, soon became a large part of his civilian life.

Then there was Mommy, Nezzie Shabazz, a creative soul with a smile as bright as the sun, an only child whose mother and stepfather were socialites in their Columbus, Ohio, community.

Her mother, Inez Taylor, came from South America. Lightly complexioned with tan freckles spread across her face, she was quite beautiful. She had wavy, fire-engine red hair that was always well-coiffed. Her signature color was red—nails, lips, and even the attitude to match.

Mommy's biological father was Joseph Jackson. Grandma Inez divorced him when he was caught in an adulterous affair, and he resorted to domestic violence. Ultimately, Grandma Inez sought revenge by blowing up his car downtown, which took a portion of a government building with it. These actions landed her in jail for two years.

She then married James 'Jimmy' Taylor, who raised Mommy while Grandma Inez was focused on living the high life. James, also lightly complexioned, was every bit of the suave Renaissance man. He was tall with broad shoulders, had wavy hair, and maintained an always-manicured appearance. He worked at Ohio Bell as an electrician for over twenty years before becoming the first black supervisor.

Even though she had remarried, Grandma Inez wouldn't let a failed marriage or a daughter from that union stop her from enjoying herself. This made it particularly difficult for Mommy, who usually ended up in the back seat of a car with a box of Payday candy bars and a Coca-Cola, while her mother lived it up at supper clubs with several bottles of expensive champagne lining the tables or at Eastern Star meetings with other socialites who considered themselves the black bourgeoisie.

Despite Grandma Inez's lavish lifestyle, she and Grandpa Jimmy had an electric relationship—he was as handsome as she was beautiful, and they both embodied the same spirit of hardworking determination. Externally, they succeeded in living the coveted 'American Dream' in an era when African Americans rising through the ranks was fraught with peril. She was a nurse assistant with a side hustle as a dressmaker; she was determined to rise above the rest. Similarly, he also had a strong work ethic, which allowed him to move up in his company's ranks. A powerhouse team, they owned both a coal yard and a cleaning business. They succeeded financially despite racism, classism, sexism, and any other type of -ism that stood in their way.

Grandma Inez wasn't just a skilled worker, though. She was also an equestrienne and an excellent markswoman. Her father was said to be a Prince Hall Mason, a farmer, and a skillful gunman who owned slaves. He had always wanted a son to raise up in the family trade. As fate would have it, though, he had a girl. To assuage the disappointment of not having someone to carry on the family name, he poured his life into his daughter. This was a great benefit to Grandma Inez in the long run, although she personally felt it was a form of abandonment.
Despite these feelings, her experiences nevertheless translated into suave business acumen, which allowed her to become a proud asset to Grandpa Jimmy.

Externally, life was grand. Internally, though, when they came home and closed the door to their lovely house on 988 East Rich Street, walking distance from Ohio Avenue Elementary where Mommy attended, the atmosphere was undesirable. As Mommy grew up, each year the story became clearer. Grandpa Jimmy, who was kind, protective, and gentle with Mommy, was often drunk on the weekends, a womanizer, and a wife beater. This was a spousal pattern that Inez couldn't seem to break in her life. This marriage also ended in divorce.

And as her mother and father rubbed shoulders with the who's who of the socialite community, Mommy grew up an only child. She was spoiled even by today's standards, though. She told me once her favorite shoes were from Capezio and she had every color they produced. She grew up with many pets, but her favorite was a rabbit with big floppy ears, like the kind you might see at a state fair. Her love for creativity was inspired by Grandma Inez, who actually made a lot of their clothing and the draperies that hung in their extravagant home. Mommy even worked one of her first jobs in a drapery workroom, where she developed a deep love for creating home interiors.

But at twenty years old, and as a single woman with no prospects for a husband, Mommy was considered an old maid by Grandma and her friends. All of the girls Mommy knew were already married or engaged. So, as not to disappoint her mother, she did what any respectable young woman would do. She frequented the local Non-Commissioned Officers club, where many military men were looking for wives during the Vietnam War era. And that's where Daddy found her, ripe for the picking.

From these two very different backgrounds, Daddy and Mommy crossed paths. They were shaped by their environments, their parents, and their own choices. The posterity of abuse they both experienced—emotional, physical, and psychological, whether through intention or neglect—was the fruit that could not be ignored by the tree.

The Fight

Moving to Tulsa was no different than moving to any other city we lived in. There never seemed to be any real plan of action, no solid explanations, though Mommy often said that God showed her our next home. She and Daddy would inform us of their decision within a week or so of the move, so we felt we never had enough time to say our goodbyes. Me and Tony had no say in the matter, of course, other than to tell our friends some lame reason we were leaving, like, "Daddy accepted a new job, so we have to move," or "My grandma is ill and we have to be near her." I would say anything to sound like I knew exactly what was going on. Heck, even as an adult looking back, I still can't say I have all of the answers.

Despite the unknowns at the time, though, I knew I couldn't risk telling anyone what I did know for certain: our parents couldn't make up their minds on what stability would look like for our family.

Mommy always assured us, "Everything will be better on the other side."

To that, I would think, *Better than what?* How is abruptly leaving my few friends here in Springfield better than leaving my first set of friends and Grandma in Columbus? What would be better than leaving my friends in Cincinnati? Leaving for Tulsa might have been in my parents' best interests, but not mine.

This makes me think of the elementary school I used to go and of the stenographer's pad that my classmates and Mrs. Wakeley gave me as a going-away gift before we moved to Tulsa. I guess you could say I have a lot of precious memories of these younger years. After everything I've experienced, I've learned not to take anything for granted.

I remember Clifton Elementary was a beautiful school that sat on top of a hill and looked like the United States Capitol. It had three stories and a basement and was a weathered, light-grey building with a roof of terracotta shingles and copper that had turned green through the years. The front of the building had four massive columns evenly spaced with banners of school pride hanging between them. A flagpole and an offset walkway led the way from the edge of the street to the front doors near the office. The school grounds were immaculately kept, trees and bushes perfectly manicured. Walking to school was an easy fifteen-minute walk from the house we rented. It was a straight shot. Even now, I bet I could walk it blindfolded. Go out the door, turn left, walk to the light, which is half a block away. Cross the street, walk up the hill past all the houses nestled closely together, and Clifton stands proudly at the top, ready for students to fill its halls.

The stenographer's pad was a simple gift that meant the world to me, a special memory that stayed with me as I got older. I don't know whose idea it really was at the time, but I had never received anything so affirming. Mrs. Wakeley and my classmates wrote some of the most encouraging words on those pages, each penning something about me they liked, and my heart swelled with joy with each sentiment. I never knew that I had made an impact on anybody. Even at that young age, I was so desperate for someone to notice me, and this stenographer's pad, filled with words of warm kindness, validated my existence. I had been accepted. But the feeling of belonging was cut short. I had grabbed everything but that pad when I had been cleaning out my desk and preparing to go. The day of our move, I desperately begged Daddy for us to go and retrieve it, but he didn't want to go back. Yet my pad wasn't the only thing that got left behind.

So did the potential to be a normal kid, in a normal school, with normal teachers and a normal life.

Although my time at Clifton was relatively idyllic, it wasn't perfect. I had my share of fights, too. As something that became a familiar pattern in my childhood, I went through my rites of passage as the new kid on the block—which eventually led to a fight between me and an obviously distraught girl who, along with her unruly entourage, would follow me down the hill day after day. They would taunt me and laugh at me scornfully, causing me to run home in tears, and I was tired of their cruel words and mean laughter. Rumor had it that I was going to be taught a lesson, but for what, I sure didn't know.

That day I dealt with the bully was like most days at Clifton Elementary. My classmates, a rowdy group of third, fourth, and fifth graders, were becoming restless in their seats since it was Friday. With the school bell poised to ring in only a few minutes, our homeroom teacher, Mrs. Wakeley, reminded us of the special project due on Monday.

Mrs. Wakeley was a very thin, white lady who sometimes wore long jean skirts and high-neck blouses with lacy collars that were clasped with pearly buttons. Her sweaters had some of the most interesting designs on them and often emulated the seasons we were in or the holiday that was the closest. Sometimes, her collars had itty bitty pearls nicely arranged on them, sewn into place by a skilled factory worker. Her face was thin, and her lips were always the same dusty rose color as they were the day before. The blush she wore was a bit too bright for her fair skin, but at least you always knew where her cheeks were. Her strawberry-blonde hair had gentle highlights and was fanned out into a mass of soft, curly waves. Her eyes were the most peculiar shade of aqua blue that I'd ever seen.

Mrs. Wakeley was a woman who was mild-mannered, patient, and kind; I respected her warmth and how she took time to help each of us, no matter what subject we were struggling with—I wanted to be just like her. She was also very organized. Her desk had everything neatly arranged, including a coffee cup she would sip from that was always within arm's reach. She taught English and had the best chalkboard penmanship that I had ever seen. Each sentence she wrote, I carefully mimicked in my notebook. I really admired her handwriting so much that I made it my own.

When the bell finally rang, class had ended. I gathered my belongings from my desk and put them in my butterfly-decorated backpack, feeling a knot form in my stomach as I anticipated the cruel taunts that awaited me. I shook my head. No, I wouldn't let fear get me.

One of my newest friends, Genesis Henderson, who must've

been how Jayne Kennedy looked as a fourth grader, leaned over while I put the last of my things in my backpack and whispered, "I would walk home with you, but my mom picks me up and she'd get worried."

I chuckled at Genesis' slight lisp, which always made me smile.

"What is it, Keeya?" she asked, a stunned look on her face as I began to laugh *so* much that I actually had a tear in my eye. "Keeya, you are so silly," she quipped, shaking her head as she packed her backpack and stood up to go to the dismissal line.

I pushed in my chair immediately, ready to follow, and earned a stern look from Mrs. Wakeley for the obnoxious scraping sound my chair had made. Although I cringed at her disapproval, nothing could dampen the enthusiasm inside: not only was I ready for the weekend, but I was ready to face the bullies who had spread the rumor that I would get beat up today after school.

I moved through the line and out of the side door, where we were dismissed. I turned around and waved to Genesis as she jumped into her mom's car and drove away from my sight.

I tried to walk as fast as possible, excited thoughts racing through my mind. I wished that Tony didn't go to another school because he would have protected me from these mean kids. I had told him about the rumor, and he had encouraged me not to back down. He had reminded me of my wins in other fights, how Kosi Harris trained me in Taekwondo, and how capable I was of defending myself. And while I had convinced myself I felt ready to take these kids on, now that the dreaded time was looming nearer, my confidence was beginning to have second thoughts.

I sped up my pace through the grass, hoping the bullies had forgotten about me, but that had just been wishful thinking. Sure enough, there was the girl and her posse waiting for me at the bottom of the hill, blocking the path between me and home. My stomach tightened; butterflies were fighting in a chaotic swirl in the pit of my stomach now. As I drew closer, I felt myself getting angry about how tired I was of going through this stupid ritual. Rude kids, no matter what city I moved to, seemed to have the same goal of terrorizing the new girl at school.

I noticed there were actually more kids than usual and some were eating snacks they had obviously forgotten to eat at lunchtime. What was this—a boxing match? I was disgusted at the fact that the motley bunch was excited to see someone get hurt. I had no intention of being someone's entertainment. But there was no time for this type of thinking. I had to defend myself, and there was no turning back.

The black girl who stepped forward from the loosely scattered group of kids looked poorly kept based on the appearance of her clothes. Although we were the same height, I also noticed her large forehead, which sported a semi-healed scab that may have happened from some other scuffle, and her hair, initially sectioned into braided pigtails, had come unraveled at some point during the day.

She began yelling at me about how stupid I was, and the next thing I knew, kids had formed a circle around us. Encouraged, she screamed out slurs, insults I could barely make out due to her heavy ghetto-speaking style. But understanding what my opponent said didn't seem to matter once she shoved me to the ground.

At that moment, I felt something inside of me snap. I remember leaving my backpack on the ground, the V-shaped butterflies glinting in the light—then I lunged at her like an alley cat and punched her as hard as I could in the face. My taut fist collided with her teeth, but I didn't stop. I quickly followed up with another blow. Dimly, I was aware of everyone screaming, giving high fives, laughing at us while we scuffled on the sidewalk. We rolled into the bushes next to someone's driveway, which allowed me to begin to get the best of her. With one swift punch, I bloodied her nose and she began to cry.

I did it!

One of the boys, who must have been her brother, jumped in to break us up. He lifted my arm to declare me the winner as the girl stumbled to her feet. Crying uncontrollably, she burst through the crowd toward her home. He looked at me after she had left and said, "Girl, you got heart!"

My adrenaline still pumping strong, I snatched my arm away from him, disgusted. I picked up my backpack, pushed through the onlookers, and hurried home.

I couldn't wait to tell Tony that I'd won the fight!

As my mind began to clear and the adrenaline ebbed away, I looked at my knuckles and noticed one was bleeding; my face, also, stung with scratches the girl had inflicted. As I passed house after house, I began to cry silently.

I had won the fight, but I was tired of having to prove myself. I couldn't wait to get home to Mommy. I needed a hug.

Tulsa

The night Mommy told us of their decision was like every other night in our family. We were eating dinner, sitting on the cold floor with a blanket spread out underneath the three of us. Daddy was absent, which was no surprise. The radiator, which Mommy had just turned on, began to warm up, allowing blessed heat to fill the room. I recall I scooted closer to the radiator and looked up at Mommy's towering figure, noting from her expression that something was wrong. She had been moping around all day, which was how I knew sad news was coming.
Bowing her head, she spoke in a lowered tone, "We're moving in a few weeks." Stunned, I looked at Tony for his reaction. He merely continued to chew his food.
Nothing ever seemed to faze him.

I stared down at my plate and began to play with my peas as Mommy laid out the plans for how we would pack and say goodbye to everyone at the church and at our schools. While our parents had given us three weeks' notice this time, it didn't make me feel much better. Tears began to well up in my eyes as I took another bite of cold peas, feeling their buttery taste on my tongue.
I looked up at Mommy, half-chewed food still in my mouth, and asked,

"Why, Mommy?

I don't want to move. I want to stay at this school with my friends."

With an understanding sincerity, she came close to me and slowly rubbed my shoulder, answering, "I know, dear."

I shrugged out from under her touch. I didn't want to be comforted. I wanted this whole conversation to stop!

There were only four months left in the school year—just four months. And besides, my birthday was coming up and I had wanted to bring cookies to school to celebrate with everyone. I had wanted to be in the play that we were rehearsing for school. And what about spending the summer with my friends?

I became furious inside, but I found all I could do was cry. I sniffled and rubbed my runny nose. The peas by this time had turned to a slimy mush, so I spit them out on a napkin. I glanced up to see how Tony fared and I was only half-surprised to see he had already gathered his dishes and was going to the kitchen to clean up.

"Where are we moving to?" I demanded.

"Tulsa, Oklahoma," she answered in a matter-of-fact tone.

At her reply, my tears gave way to small, hiccupping sobs. After I scraped my plate and put it in the sink, I retreated down the hallway to my room. After what Mommy had just told us, I welcomed the comfort of my bed and eventually drifted to sleep.

With each passing day, my heart grew colder toward my parents. With Daddy being an over-the-road truck driver, he was never home much. Usually when our family had to move, Mommy was given the task of breaking the news to us, and then Daddy would come into town to help us pack.

When I finally told Mrs. Wakeley we were leaving, it was my last day at Clifton Elementary School. She broke the news to the class during the last period.

Genesis was so sad. We cried bitterly and hugged each other tightly.

"Keeya, you are my best friend," she declared sincerely, "and always remember that! And don't ever forget me, okay?"

Her lisps usually made me smile, but this time I couldn't smile at all.

Mrs. Wakeley gently interrupted our conversation to bring me to the front of the class. "Class, may I have your attention, please?" she announced. "Let's make sure today that we all sign this stenographer's pad and leave a special comment for Keeya to remember us by."

I was in shock at her words. They were going to do that for me? Never had I felt so important before.

The pad went around from child to child, and I smiled when I collected the pad from the last person. By the time I returned to my desk, I was simply beaming. I sat down and read through every comment and signature; each word was special to me. Then class resumed and it was time for me to get my things from my desk, pack up, and go home. We were leaving for Tulsa in a couple of days and there was still so much left to do at home.

Genesis helped me clear my belongings out of my cubby space and my desk, with other students pitching in to help. I held on tightly to my stenographer's pad until I realized that I wanted to run and give Mrs. Wakeley a big hug. I put the pad on my desk chair and darted over to her. I hugged her so suddenly and tightly that I almost knocked her down. She merely laughed and sent me back for my things so that I could be in the dismissal line before the bell rang.

My emotions were swirling inside of me like a windstorm as I walked down the familiar hallway, down the traveled steps, and through the often-used side door. I waved one last time to Genesis as she hopped in her mom's car, and she waved goodbye and blew me kisses until I couldn't see her anymore.

After she disappeared from view, I wondered if this was all a bad dream somehow—that I would wake up and we wouldn't be moving and I'd still be with Genesis and Mrs. Wakeley and the rest of my friends.

The weekend was filled with trips to the store to buy tape and boxes. Mommy had had us collect boxes from the local businesses several days ago, but we still needed more. When Monday rolled around, we were all set.

Then I remembered.

"Wait!" I yelled, just as we were heading out of the front door. "Daddy, I left my stenographer pad at school!"

Daddy, shaking his head, answered, "That's too bad. We're

running behind schedule and we're already two hours behind. I have a short run I gotta take in between, so too bad for your paper."

"It's not just paper, Daddy," I explained, hands balling into fists. "The kids at school gave it to me as a going-away present. I need to go and get it. *Please?*"

"Keeya, I'm sorry, but we don't have time," he replied firmly. And that was that.

I was sad about my stenographer's pad. I could picture it on my chair, right where I had so hastily left it. Would my classmates find it and realize I'd left it behind?

I was angry at Mommy and Daddy, but I knew I couldn't protest or Daddy's patience would begin to wear thin.

Daddy motioned for Tony and me to get in the truck. While Daddy turned on the vehicle and slowly switched gears, I looked outside the window, memorizing the scenery. Ebenezer Baptist Church, which needed so many repairs done to its exterior, held some of the most amazing memories of Tony preaching his first sermon at the age of fourteen. The convenience store where I'd 'borrowed' Daddy's coins for a frozen chocolate malt that I could remember vividly—the cold gritty grains of expired chocolate and the sticky seal that I carefully peeled away each time I would indulge. On the right was the barber shop where Tony would occasionally get a haircut. I loved to go there just to eat the strawberry foil candies, the ones with the hard exterior and ooey-gooey insides. We bumped along down the street, headed toward our new destination, but as I took in the familiar scenes, my thoughts returned to the pad that sat on my chair that would never be claimed.

Eventually, we arrived to Tulsa in Daddy's eighteen-wheeler semi-truck he'd leased from Robert's Express (a trucking company he worked many years for) and without very much money. Since we had no place to live, Tony and I were dropped off at a library downtown while Mommy and Daddy found us a place for the night. This usually meant a local shelter for Mommy and Tony and me while Daddy slept in the truck at a local truck stop.

The only things Tony and I had to eat while at the library were two, big multi-colored suckers with the colors twisting and turning into each other layer by layer. These were the kind you could get at a carnival set up in a vacant parking lot or at a state fair. Oh, how I wished we were together at a fair, enjoying our suckers like normal people!

Instead, I was bewildered, sad in a new city where we didn't know anyone. To be completely honest, I was so afraid of what would become of us that I had to swallow back tears for fear of alerting library patrons of our situation. I couldn't do that—blow our cover—so I held my sucker and tried to enjoy it.

Who knew if Mommy would be successful in finding us a place for the night or not?

We were at the library for hours, catching up on comic books or any titles that piqued our interest. As the sun dipped below the horizon, I began to feel anxious, concerned about what might happen to us since our parents had not returned yet.

As usual, with the quiet reliability of an older sibling, Tony comforted me and reassured me everything would be okay. I decided, being weary from the journey and hungry from the lack of food, to pester him. But, not to be deterred, he remained patient with me as time stretched on and on.

I couldn't determine if Tony was okay with everything happening or not. In times like these, he seemed to come to Earth from another planet, where he was trained to engage these circumstances with the gift of silence. While I found myself emotionally distraught, he always seemed to know what to do. I admired his resolve in the face of uncertainty and wanted to be able to respond like that, too.

Tony was an exceptional kid who was quite mature beyond his years. He had to be this way, since our parents seemed incapable of recognizing the damage their decisions had on the family. He often told me stories to take our minds off everything we endured. He took his responsibility seriously…too seriously, in fact. At the age of sixteen, he was still nursing ulcers that occurred years prior and was often depressed, but he always had a smile for me. It was like he knew he was our only hope at normalcy.

Tears formed in my eyes at the setting sun and I asked, "Where are they, Tony? Don't they know we're hungry?"

He answered with an uncertainty that he tried to hide, "They'll be back for us soon, Keeya."
"But, Tony, I'm hungry."

So, he reached into the pocket of his jeans and pulled out a piece of Juicy Fruit gum that he got from Daddy the day before. The wrapper was stuck to the gum and a little bit of lint lined the zig-zag edges. He tried to pick off what he could and gave the sweet to me.

I chewed it and found satisfaction in his attempt to comfort me. By this time, we had been sitting on a bench inside the library for several minutes. Once or twice, I'd glimpsed staff members stealing glances at us, the kids who were obviously there alone.

Finally, just before the head librarian expressed concern over us, I looked up and saw Mommy searching the aisles for us. I bolted toward her and yelled, "Mommy!"
Embarrassed by my exuberance, she embraced me and asked, "Where is Tony?" "He's coming," I said.

Tony walked up with his head down and a sullen expression on his face, trying to mask the relief I know he must've felt. He looked at Mommy knowingly and asked, "So, where is the shelter?"

Surprised at him, Mommy answered, "It's a wonderful place, really. There are a lot of other kids there, and tasty food, too."

With that explanation, we walked out of the library and got into an unfamiliar van, where two ladies greeted us. They were from a local church. They had received the call earlier that day and helped Mommy find a shelter that would take us in.

We stayed at the shelter for thirty days while Daddy continued working for the trucking company. When it was time to leave, we moved into a decent two-story apartment. Down the hill in the backyard was an old playground where lots of kids of all ages played. Aware that this was to be our new home until my parents decided otherwise, I staunchly decided that I would go outside every day until I found someone to be my new friend. And it didn't take long for me to discover summertime in Tulsa was much hotter than in Springfield either!

One sweltering day, I got up, dressed, and went outside. At the playground, there was a girl playing with other kids and she seemed a bit older than the rest. Maybe older than I was. She seemed a bit bossy, but friendly.
Catching sight of me, she asked, "Are you new to the neighborhood?"

I replied, the worn words rolling easily off my tongue, "Yes, I have an older brother, and my mom doesn't work. My dad drives trucks and he's not home a lot."

"Cool. Well, if you need a friend, I'm the one. I know everyone, and nobody messes with me. My name's Tanika." She gave me a broad, confident smile.
After that, we immediately became friends.

Tanika came from a big family. Her mother was a single mom, who became like a second parent to me, and her dad was in her life but not a lot. Tanika also had a younger sister and brother. Her best friend was Shelby, a girl next door who was staying with her aunt for the summer. Both Tanika and Shelby were considered 'fast friends' by Mommy's standards, who preferred I develop friendships more carefully, but she caved in to my desire for friends since she felt bad for the life we lived.

When I think about it, it's weird how quickly people's lives change. Take my parents, for instance. Daddy went to college and studied English. He wanted to become an English teacher, but he was drafted to fight in the Vietnam War. Mommy, in contrast, was a skilled seamstress and grew up well-to-do. They met each other in the late '60s at an Officers club in Columbus, Ohio. He was part of a singing group that toured the clubs when he was not on duty in the Air Force.

Soon after they met, Mommy became pregnant with Tony. She married Daddy to save face—and her mother's, too. It was said that Grandma Inez, who was from South America, put a double-barreled shotgun to his face, lifted his chin, and warned him not to make her look bad. The marriage took place before Christmas in 1969, and Tony was born in January. Then when they were stationed at Torrejón Air Base in Madrid, Spain, in 1975, I was born in March.

During their young marriage, Mommy developed fibroid tumors in her uterus, which landed her in the hospital frequently. She eventually stayed home and offered her services to local decorators, a growing business that received the attention of local newspapers and a few Christian television shows on the Trinity Broadcasting Network.

Unfortunately, their marital problems magnified when Daddy became jealous of Mommy's success. The specific issues the two of them had were complicated at best, though I never knew all the details. I only heard bits and pieces of arguments. Usually late at night, there were yells and screams, followed by Mommy's sobbing. The confusion of their relationship only added to the disillusionment of the situation. I could never figure out why anyone would want to live this way.

And now here we were in Tulsa. During this time, I was entering my formative pre-teen years. I became defiant with Mommy, and that summer I got into more trouble than ever. My friendships with Tanika and Shelby deepened, and there were many poorly supervised sleepovers at their houses—leading to delightful naughtiness with their male cousins. The neighborhood boys also knew us. Although we weren't totally bad, we joyfully pushed the limits. For example, we once engaged in a contest to see who could kiss the most boys without getting caught. I won first place, Tanika was runner-up, and Shelby came in last. I tried to hide my willful activities from Tony, but like a hawk after a field mouse, he was always onto me.

Ironically, we faithfully attended Destination Discovery, which was a mission to reach inner city kids with the gospel of Jesus. We were also very active at Victory Christian Center with Pastor Billy Joe Daugherty. I attended early morning prayer at 5 a.m. with a group of black families who lived in our neighborhood. In public, around my parents and other adults, I was an angel, always polite, friendly, and well-spoken, behavior that differed from my wilder activities.

Fall came too quickly, and it was time to go to school. That's when I decided that I really liked Tulsa and didn't want to move anymore. Why should I? I had grown to enjoy my new life here. My relationship with Tony, as a result, became a bit strained. He often caught me in lies and warned me not to become like Tanika. I defended my friend, realizing that I was actually worse than her in behavior. Tony, in sharp contrast to me, had become more serious about church and all things Jesus.

Yet while I also went to church faithfully, I had questions about my family's situation. I wondered why God would allow Daddy to belittle and beat Mommy and Tony. I wondered why God didn't stop us from moving all of the time. I was tired of leaving teachers and friends I loved so much. If God loved me so much, like they told me in youth group at the Mabee Center, why didn't He stop all of this from happening to our family?

When Tony and I finished our respective grades in the spring, Mommy decided to pull us out of public school. After watching countless hours of Christian television, I remember having watched a program with Mommy once about parents who decided to homeschool their children to shield them from the increasingly wicked and carnal world. Perhaps this was what had motivated her. I cringed whenever I watched this show because I knew how Mommy received it. I saw the look on her face and I knew that she saw me in decline. It's not that she didn't know that I was slipping away, but she was afraid to confront my behavior and push away one of my only friends.

In the coming weeks, I begged my parents to no avail for them to let me be normal for once. I was met with very rote answers, like, "It will be good for you both, Keeya," and "We know that you don't understand right now, but you will thank us in the future."

Mommy usually conveyed her feelings to me as kindly as she could, but I sensed she was overprotective of me. Not so much with Tony, though. Mommy seemed to treat him differently, maybe because he was five years older and a boy. She seemed to depend on him as if he didn't need the same type of protection. In fact, he seemed to be *her* protection. Despite this, I felt that Mommy's treatment of Tony was unfair because who would allow him to be a kid? Where was his protection? When would he feel what I felt from him—that he had a place to run to when Daddy was railing both accusations and his fists?

Then there was Daddy. He basically went along with what Mommy wanted and didn't care much about us being homeschooled as long as he didn't have to do it. He was a long-distance truck driver, which meant he didn't see us very much anyway. He could have been home more but he was not happy there. He had more important things to do, like visit women in other states or whatever he did on those long-distance runs. Maybe that's what some of their fights were about? Who knows.

When he wasn't drinking or high, Daddy actually was very likeable to an extent. He was always jesting and making a spectacle of himself and others who were around him. He could also sing in a way that captured my heart. However, despite this easygoing nature, Daddy had a temper that usually ruined most attempts at normalcy or being in a public place with him.

Everyone walked on eggshells in his presence, never knowing when he would turn into Mr. Hyde. He often behaved with a paranoia that only he understood. He would peer out of the living room blinds. Close the door behind him, then open it and look out of it again, only to shut it and mutter something to himself that no one could make out. Other times, he would accuse someone in the house of doing something wrong. When he acted like this, we knew to get out of his way. Usually, the accused would suffer being smacked or belittled to the point of tears.

I often wondered if his behavior was a result of being in Vietnam or from growing up in Cabrini-Green or from the five foster homes he lived in as a youngster in Chicago. I once heard that his own mother tried to sleep with him. Whatever it was, I knew that he was a badly damaged man.

I tried to relate to him by being silly, cracking jokes, and reading books that I felt would impress him. I would even try to sing a song or spell a difficult word to hopefully gain his approval, but it was impossible to please him. He seemed more preoccupied with his terrible relationship with Mommy than to bother getting to know who his children were.

Instability—mental, emotional, and physical—was commonplace in our home. It seemed to me like the only thing constant was unexpected change. I longed to know what it was like to live in one city, grow up in one neighborhood, and have family reunions, family vacations, and other *normal* family times my friends seemed to enjoy. Just when I was comfortable living in a new city, Mommy would break the news to me and Tony that we were moving. When we asked why we were moving, her answers always seemed vague and over my head, and this continued pattern left me uneasy.

The next year seemed to be the worst one ever for me. Tony, tired of his life at home, got his GED and applied for a technical school in Dallas, Texas. He was accepted and made plans to leave home for the first time. I was outwardly happy for him but inwardly devastated—what would I do without him? He was my rock in this crazy, unpredictable family.

I had no choice but to accept the natural progression of things. Why *wouldn't* Tony leave and go to college? Hadn't he experienced enough heartache? Wasn't he deserving of normalcy in his life? He did his best to shield me from hardships, but didn't *he* deserve a chance to have peace?

I remember one day he bought me a really nice duffel bag in green, my favorite color.

Because it came from him, I treasured his gift. It went with me to every sleepover. I even remember when he bought me my first rap tape. We weren't allowed to listen to secular music, but it didn't stop Tony from bringing home Salt-N-Pepa's *Hot, Cool, & Vicious* album. When we were much younger, Tony would crank up the radio when Mommy and Daddy weren't there and practice breakdancing. Sometimes, he would forget himself and Mommy would catch him practicing and ask him what he was doing. We would look at each other, and then he would explain that he was exercising. We would later get a good laugh over his little white lie.

  When Tony had his first job at a little burger joint called B&F Express, almost all of his money went to pay the bills, bills that Daddy should have been paying. But the lack never added up. With Daddy as an over-the-road truck driver, we should have had more to work with. Mommy was often stressed, robbing Peter to pay Paul. Even with her sewing business taking off, there still wasn't enough. Tony was such a loyal son. He didn't ask questions. He just signed over paycheck after paycheck. He gave everything he had to keep the peace in the family and take care of me and Mommy.

  And with the little money remaining, Tony managed to purchase a used Porsche 914. It cost twenty-four hundred dollars—and that was how he earned his freedom. One day, he loaded up his black-and-white car, ready to head to Dallas. Before leaving, he looked at Mommy and said, "I love you, Mama," and gave her a tender hug.

He hugged Daddy, and then he looked over at me and said, "Take care of yourself, Keeya...and stay out of trouble."

With tears streaming down my face, I asked him, "Who's going to hug me when I'm scared?"

To this he replied, "You're going to have to learn to hug yourself." He reached down and gave me a hug and a kiss on the forehead. Then he got into his car and drove off.

That was a day I would never forget.

Later that year, perhaps because Tony had left, Daddy begged for forgiveness for the life he was leading and the trouble that the family experienced at his hands. He made promises and said he'd never hit Mommy again. Tears flowed from every face in the room. It was a hopeful time for us back then.

Unfortunately, such peaceful resolution didn't last long enough. It was the same year that a well-known televangelist confessed his adulterous relationship with a prostitute. This was a man our family watched regularly on TV, especially when he would sing, "There is Room at the Cross for You". Mommy and I would draw close to each other and praise God together with him.

The shocking news of the affair seemed to shake Daddy to his core, though, and he was brought to tears. Unfortunately, the whole thing became too much for him to handle. By Christmas, Daddy sat me and Mommy down. What he said fertilized a small seed of hatred in my heart.

"Keeya, I want you to call your friends and tell them that you are moving. We're going to Dallas."

This one caught me by surprise, leaving me stunned. I finally exclaimed, "But, Daddy, I'm tired of moving. It seems like we move every two weeks!"

This made him angry. He shouted, "Don't talk back to me, girl, and do as you are told.

I'm the man in this house! Who are you to question me?"

I cried and ran to my room. I knew talking to Mommy would only further upset the situation. I wanted to call Tony. I wished he was there to tell me that everything would be okay. Then I remembered what he told me about hugging myself and I tried to be a big girl about it. For the first time, I sucked it up and called Tanika.

The phone rang, and she answered.

Why do I always have to do this? I thought, biting my lip.

"Tanika," I said slowly, my words sounding flat to my ears, "I have something to tell you." My hand gripped the receiver tightly. "W- we are moving."

Tanika protested, "But it's Christmas time and we're going to my aunt and uncle's to celebrate and have Christmas dinner! I was going to ask your mom if you could come." The disappointment in her voice cut me inside.

I found I couldn't answer. Instead, tears formed and rolled down my face, soaking into the neckline of my t-shirt.

She was quiet for a moment, then asked, "When are you moving?" "This week."

There was silence on the phone at first, and then as we began to say our goodbyes, I could hear the quiver in her voice.

Life Happens to Us All

Hot tears of disappointment glided down the face of a once-innocent girl who, faced with the uncertainty of her journey, took the first steps toward a life that would be her own.

Despite her attempt to wipe them away, the tears returned again and again as if there was a valve in the seat of her soul encouraging their release. As she gazed out of the window, she took in the familiar scene, searching the skyscrapers for a reason to turn around. But as she came closer to the exit, a warm sense of accomplishment began to slowly grow in her heart and the tears gave way to a feeling of euphoria.

That was the beginning of an entry to my diary when I was in Dallas, when I had decided to finally do something about my situation. There was no date, just words. I often wrote my thoughts down or I would pen poems that were mostly left unfinished.

The day before we abruptly left for Dallas, Mommy had been crying all day as we packed up the rest of our things. We sold a lot of things and gave the rest away. Mommy still had fabrics of unfinished projects for customers, material that we strapped above the cramped bed space in the cab of the truck. When I saw those sheets, all I could think of was how Daddy became jealous of Mommy's success and would often knock her down to size with an occasional beating. Over the course of a year, just to spite her, he even drained her bank account of over ninety thousand dollars. Mommy may've been publicly successful with her business, but she was privately broken.

The night before we left, I could hear them arguing. I pictured Daddy standing over Mommy as he was yelling like a madman. I could always hear her crying, "But, Robert, why?" When the yelling subsided, I could hear Mommy weeping. Daddy opened the bedroom door and went downstairs. I assumed he went to drink, which he did a lot to calm himself down.

Day after day and night after night, we were in the back as Daddy drove from city to city and from state to state, the fabrics for Mommy's customers hanging over us. She would often look at them as they swung back and forth and sob deeply. She was a great businesswoman at the top of her game, engineering draperies and pillows and like things for the homes of her customers. Her clients, in turn, had often invited us to lunch or dinner and I witnessed them sing her praises. But all that was left of her success was above her, swaying with the thuds and bumps of the eighteen-wheeler. A constant reminder of the cruelty we had to endure at the hands of my father. And it didn't seem to bother him at all. He seemed satisfied that he had overpowered Mommy, content that she no longer had a business to speak of.

In total, we spent nearly eight or nine months living out of that back cab. I turned thirteen on the road.

Daddy's job required him to travel almost all of the forty-eight states, which he would use to deliver loads of 'goods' as I later found out. It was against his contract to have people travel with him without permission, but we were essentially homeless. He had blown so much money on drugs and parties that we had nowhere to go. I remember hiding in the cab area, which was the size of a twin-size mattress, where I would put a cup or books and little toiletries for the journey; we each had several bags of clothing and personal items that were stored inside spaces on the outside of the cab. We had to hide when we arrived at Department of Transportation checkpoints and delivery sites.

As we drove on and on, I found I resented being homeschooled because it was just another way I was trapped with this family. Who wanted to learn from parents who couldn't provide stability? I missed my friends and I missed just living and sleeping in my own bed. I wanted to have a normal life, not be stuck on the road with no end in sight. I cried more during that time than I had ever cried before. My tears created a place in my heart that harbored a vendetta. I wanted Daddy to feel fear, like the kind he had created in us, for so long that I began to desire his death. I fantasized about him having a heart attack or waking up one morning and he would just drop dead. I had nightmares of murdering him.

I hated Daddy so much back then for what he constantly did to us.

Occasionally, we would visit Tony, and those meetings were always so intense. Tony, by now, continued to attend school and learn how to do technical things with video. Daddy would often tell us that he was going to beat his son up since Tony was proving to be successfully independent, an adult. Mommy confided to me she believed Daddy was jealous of everybody. I couldn't understand why Daddy was so angry all of the time. Why couldn't he be proud of his son and his accomplishments like Mommy was? I couldn't figure out how Daddy came to the conclusions that he did. It never seemed to make sense. Why would he be so mad at Tony, who was a peaceful, loving, and kind person? My brother was a young Christian man who was good and funny and never got into the trouble that was typical for his age. He was never disrespectful to Daddy, no matter how many insults he endured. So, aware of the tension in the family, Mommy would always plead with Daddy to let us have a peaceful visit.

For me, visiting Tony was something that always lifted my spirits. He frequently spoiled me with candy or chips or anything he had to give me. I knew how much he loved me and how sorrowful he was that my life was what it was. Tony seemed to be doing well in his studies, which made me happy. He had friends and a car, and he didn't have to put up with Daddy unless we came into town. It was unfortunate that Mommy and I couldn't live in Tony's dorm with his roommate.

One day on the road, Mommy was in the back while I sat in the front seat next to Daddy, who was driving. I faced him with my anger toward him burning inside of me. I guess my feelings were as plain as day on my face.

He looked at me, a dark, dry smile on his lips.

"Yeah, little girl, you're looking at me like you hate me. Well, I'm used to it! Everyone since my mama has given me that look."

I looked away as we pulled into a rest stop. I thought about what he said, and my hot face flushed with a mixture of fear and rage.

He pushed the air brake, which made its usual loud noise. He looked back over at me and how I'd propped my bare feet up on the dashboard.

Daddy sneered, "You look like a call girl, sitting up there mad." I felt his callous words stab my heart.

I glared at him and screamed, "Why would you say that to me? I hate you!"

Always with a ready answer, he spat back, "I'm used to it, Keeya. What else you got?"

I opened the door to get out of the truck, just barely missing a punch he had thrown. The sudden momentum caused me to fall to the ground.

Mommy came from the back, exclaiming, "Baby, are you okay?"

I just sat there, watching as Daddy jumped down and came around the front of the cab toward me. Seeing him loom over me, I covered my face and braced myself.

But the blows never came.

Not far away, tourists and other truck drivers walked by and milled about. Glancing at the passers-by, Daddy changed his mind and strode for the men's restroom; at the entrance, he looked back at me and shook his head.

I got back into the truck and crawled into the back and cried. I lay next to Mommy, who held me close. In the quiet of her arms, I whispered, "I hate him, Mommy."

"Me, too, baby," she whispered back. "Me, too."

Under the shadow of such instability, when I was in my mid-teens, I made up my mind that I no longer had to suffer for the ill-calculated consequences of my parents' decisions nor endure the judgment of my well-meaning but distant older brother. Now, my only belongings lay in the trunk of an old car belonging to my ex-boyfriend's sister, a young woman who I'd convinced to drive me to the Greyhound bus station in downtown Dallas, at the corner of Lamar and Commerce Streets. I realized that I had everything I needed—or at least I hoped so!

By the time we wheeled into the mostly vacant parking lot, I had finished writing my excited feelings in my diary and now turned my attention to the destination that came ever closer.

Carefully avoiding the numerous potholes that littered the worn pavement, Stacy parked the car and took a deep breath as she leaned back into her seat. She was a taller-than-average single mom of nineteen, a young woman who had matured too quickly with twin boys to look after. Although slightly overweight, she possessed a beauty that needed no makeup to enhance. Her skin was the color of butter pecan ice cream, and even when she was sad, her eyes always seemed to smile at you.

An outcast in her family because she had kids out of wedlock, Stacy understood pain and how life happens to us all. Her parents were prominent socialites who had a booming cosmetic company. When they learned of their daughter's situation, they chose to cut her off from the benefits of their financial success.

This was not the case with her brother, Caleb. Though slightly older than Stacy, he enjoyed their parents' success through the appearance of obedience and responsibility toward them. By doing his part, he was being groomed to run operations in the future. His loyalty to them, though, cost him his college education since he left school to dedicate himself to the family business.
I'll never forget the day I met Caleb.

At the time, I was the youngest member of Recycling Minority Business Dollars in Dallas, which held monthly meetings at RJ's by the Lake in the early '90s. I actually met his parents first. Mr. and Mrs. Hall were the epitome of class and black bourgeoisie and were the owners of Hall Cosmetics. As it turns out, they were interested in me since I had become quite the aspiring entrepreneur at the time (Mommy would have it no other way!). I remember I gave my elevator speech to try and sell them one of the Cole aquariums. After I proudly handed Mr. Hall my business card, he invited me to visit their store in Red Bird Mall.

To show I had initiative, I hopped on the bus by myself and paid them a visit one day. As I was walking through the mall, I saw Mr. Hall ahead of me with a companion and I shouted like a little kid, "Hey, there, Mr. Hall!"

I almost forgot what to say when I looked at the young man who accompanied Mr. Hall. He was about five nine or maybe five ten, light-skinned with short brown hair that had a lot of smooth waves on top. He was well-proportioned and had broad shoulders. But his eyes were the most amazing shade of chestnut brown. They sparkled and seemed to dance as he smiled.

I managed to remark to Mr. Hall that I was glad to have run into him because I couldn't find the store.

Mr. Hall chuckled and said, "This was a divine appointment, then, wasn't it?" I laughed politely and answered, "It sure is, Mr. Hall."

He looked at me and said suddenly, "Oh, forgive me, but this is my son, Caleb, who works at the store with us. He just moved back from Atlanta, where we opened another store recently."

The three of us having reached the entrance of the cosmetics store, Mr. Hall turned to Caleb, who grinned and extended his hand to me.

I quickly shook his hand and was surprised when he continued to hold my hand longer than normal. When I gave a *What are you doing?* look, he released it and slipped behind a counter to see to waiting customers.

I glanced over at Mrs. Hall, who was nearby and noticed this interaction. She merely grinned and asked if I wanted a makeover, beginning to select colors for me.

During our conversation, I occasionally glanced over at Caleb, who was busy assisting the ladies who came in and out of the store, and noted he, too, glanced back at me.

I admired the way Mrs. Hall applied my makeup, but I admired her son even more! I had never seen a young man so sophisticated—crisp white shirt, brown leather suspenders, and grey dress pants.

When my look was complete and I had chosen which products

to buy, I mentioned I would come back later.

Caleb diligently began to handwrite a receipt for me. He gave me the paper, mouthed *shhhhhh* with his finger, and smiled. Next to the list of products, he'd written, *Eyes brown, lips beautiful*. At the bottom of the receipt was his name and number.

I was floored! I was truly out of my league and I knew it, but I had to call him!

The entire bus ride back to North Dallas, I thought about Caleb. What was I going to talk about? *Hi, Mr. Sophisticated, I'm a homeschool student who's never had a real boyfriend.* How silly, I was so nervous!

Finally, I arrived home and told Mommy all about my trip to visit Mr. and Mrs. Hall. I raved about their store and how much fun my first makeover was. I told her how they gave me a free product and how Caleb had given me the receipt. We laughed and she encouraged me to call him.

Not knowing when he would be available, I called the store and he answered, "Hall Cosmetics. This is Caleb. How can I help you?"

In my most professional voice, I said, "Hi, Caleb, this is Keeya. We met earlier when your dad introduced us."

I asked when he'd get off from work. Since he'd be closing shop in a few hours, he was free to talk after nine.

"Okay, Caleb," I replied, trying to ignore the butterflies darting around in my stomach, "you can just call me after you've settled in for the night."

After receiving my number, he promised he'd call later and hung up.

I screamed all the way to Mommy, who was in the kitchen. It wasn't long before we were laughing.

"Keeya, you are so silly," she said with a disbelieving shake of her head.

"Mommy, I can't believe this!"

"What—that you have free makeup?"

"Noooo, Mommy! That he gave me his number!"

"Well, Keeya, what do you expect?" Mommy answered with an easygoing smile. "You're absolutely beautiful!"

"Aw, thank you, Mommy!"

I danced around the apartment all evening, awaiting his call. Finally, the phone rang. It was Caleb!

I learned so much about him. He had moved back home from Morehouse College to help with the family business. He had just turned twenty-one, which freaked me out a little bit. I told him that I was only fifteen, which shocked him. He felt that I was so mature for my age. We talked until I almost fell asleep on the phone. By the time I glanced over at the clock, I saw it was 1 a.m.!

Occasionally, I visited him at the store after his parents had left for the day and later we'd go to his house. It was so much fun to be around him, but I often thought of the huge age difference. I mean, six years older than me—Daddy would never allow this to go on! But

Daddy was never home long enough to know what was going on in my life. Mommy would surely never tell him that I was dating a grown man! She and I kept my relationship a secret from Daddy and even from Tony. I knew my brother would surely object to me dating someone a year older than he was.

Caleb even invited me to spend the night at his parents' home when he was house-sitting for them one time. I enjoyed exploring their house—it was a place that managed to be both luxuriously eclectic and practical at the same time. I was shocked to learn, for example, that they converted it into a warehouse for the cosmetic products they shipped and sold. The inside of their house may've looked dated, with floral motifs that were straight out of the '70s, but everything looked custom- or locally bought. It was certainly upscale—or at least compared to our budget.

Our relationship deepened as the days passed. I shared with him stories of my childhood and how abusive Daddy was. I told him all about how overprotective my brother tried to be and how much I longed for a normal life. He shared with me the difficulty of working for his parents and how he really wanted to study medicine and become a doctor. I empathized with his pain and listened closely to his thoughts and dreams. I felt like I could listen to him forever. As I got to know Caleb more and more, I realized I was falling in love with him. The thought of this scared me, but I couldn't stop. Over time, we became inseparable. He was everything that Mommy and I talked about when we spoke about my future husband!

Then there was one of those rare weekends that Daddy was home from one of his over-the-road excursions. Life was as conflicting as ever: we barely had any food in the refrigerator, Daddy argued with Mommy all evening, and I was sick of it all. It just so happened to be Halloween weekend, which we didn't celebrate, but it gave me a reason to lie and say I was going to a friend's house. And Caleb was my friend, but not the one I claimed I was going to visit.

He and I had planned to do something, you see.

I packed my bag, wishing Daddy hadn't chosen to come home then and there of all weekends. Despite my anxiety, I called Caleb at work and asked him to pick me up when he got off.
"Wait, Keeya. Isn't your father in town?" "Yes," I admitted, "but I don't want to be here."
"It's going to be after nine before I can make it over there. Are...are you sure this is

okay?"

"It's going to have to be, Caleb," I replied, "because I kind of told them I was going over to Leticia's house to spend the night."
"Okay," he finally said. "I'm on my way as soon as I close the store."

Nervous, I counted down the hours until I knew he'd be coming around. I felt bad about my parents—I had lied to them before, but not like this. This was a big step, but I could not turn back.

I had told Caleb to meet me at the entrance of the parking lot instead of by our door. As the sky was dimming from evening to night, I slipped out of the apartment and waited in the lot, glancing toward our apartment every few minutes.

If they caught me jumping into his truck, I would be so dead!

I looked at my watch in the waning light, realizing Caleb was late. Not tonight! We needed to leave ASAP—before someone saw me!

Finally, I saw his white Chevrolet Blazer turn in, the headlights shining like twin beacons. I'd never opened the door and jumped in so fast! He gave me a quick peck and we went to his apartment.

After that night, we continued to see each other. I would see his parents around town occasionally. A part of me felt like Mrs. Hall knew, but she never said anything. I was Caleb's best-kept secret.

Eventually, I met Stacy and we quickly became friends. Her life was so different from Caleb's and their parents'. While Caleb was expected to carry on the family business, Stacy was an unwed mother who struggled to make ends meet. She didn't seem to fit in at all with the family's pattern. Stacy reminded me of myself—a misfit! In her parents' eyes, she was considered an embarrassment. I definitely knew how that felt. I confided in her about my relationship with Caleb, something that we giggled about often. I think she enjoyed knowing that her brother had a secret relationship that would send their parents through the roof.

Shortly after I became acquainted Stacy, I learned about Caleb's brother, Cory, who was in the Navy. When Caleb would send care packages to Cory, I would drop a note in, too. I found out he was a part of Operation Desert Storm. I watched the news more than ever before just because of Cory; I wanted him to be okay. I wanted to finally meet him and laugh about all his stories, both serious and crazy. He had plenty, like the fact that he was a backup dancer for Vanilla Ice! He encouraged me to keep making Caleb smile, and I encouraged him that everything would be okay and that we would meet one day. I still have his letters.

No matter how close I was to this family, though, behind the scenes, I felt I would never be truly accepted by them. Not by the parents, at least, if their treatment of Stacy was any indication. There was this invisible social wall between me and them. It bothered me, but I didn't know how to address it.

As time passed, I found that I couldn't seem to get enough sleep. One Saturday, I finally woke up to find it was after two in the afternoon! I thought this was odd since I hadn't stayed up late the night before.

My lethargy went on for weeks before Caleb began to suspect something was up. And after talking with a friend one day, it dawned on me that I might be pregnant. This thought haunted me. How would this work? What would Caleb do if it was true? What would *I* do?
I had to know the truth.

Later that day, I got dressed, went to the Eckerd drug store, and bought a pregnancy test.

I opened the small box, a huge knot forming in my stomach as I followed the directions and waited.

Somehow, I knew the answer. I had read about these things. My monthly cycle had never been late before, and I couldn't seem to get enough sleep. With questions buzzing in my head, I breathed in quickly, turned around, and looked toward the counter where I had placed the long white device. It didn't take but one glance to recognize the results: one blue line and one pink blurry line.

I was definitely pregnant!

Leaving Dallas

Caleb was less than enthused at the news. In fact, he proceeded to tell me how this would ruin his life if he had a baby now. He rambled on about all the ways he would be affected, never once acknowledging that I had a life, too!

His reaction and excuses deeply angered me. I wanted a relationship, I wanted to marry him, I wanted happily ever after. Instead, I was getting rejected and my feelings were being sidelined.

But I loved him so much that I chose to grant him his wish. With one phone call, I made an appointment with the Routh Street Women's Clinic.

A week later, Caleb picked me up with the lie we were going to breakfast and then to hang out for the rest of the day. Instead, we drove down Highway 75 Central Expressway toward the clinic.

I vividly remember a line of protesters yelling at us, signs gripped in their hands; their faces were so passionate. I guess they wanted to help me, to turn us around and have us reconsider the steps we were about to take—but my loyalty to Caleb deafened me to their pleas.

One lady grabbed my arm and said firmly, "They especially want you to kill your baby."

My eyes locked with hers...and I looked away as Caleb and I walked through the entrance. As I approached the counter, the woman's words ringing in my ears, I knew this was a mistake.

While Caleb signed me in, I was emotionally numb. I stared straight ahead. "Keeya," he asked, "are you okay?"

I nodded mechanically.

Then, a woman walked up to me and escorted me into an office. She looked at me very intensely. "Keeya," she said, "I need you to do something. I need you to write a letter to your baby. This will help you bring closure to what is about to happen."

What?

Where on earth did they get this woman? I thought. *Aren't they trying to help me?* This was becoming more of a nightmare than I ever believed possible.

I took the pen I was offered and began to write my goodbyes to this unborn child. When I was finished, I handed the paper back to her.

Wordlessly, the woman escorted me back to the waiting area. "They will call your name when it's your turn."

As I sat there, I began to feel very confused. If this baby was just a blob of tissue, a fetus, and what was about to happen was merely a 'procedure', then what was the letter all about?

Stunned, I lost a sense of time.

I couldn't speak to Caleb. In fact, I hated him so much for

bringing me here. I realized that I wanted nothing more to do with him. He didn't care for me or my well-being. He only cared for himself and his reputation! Our 'party' was over, and the reality of sleeping together before marriage and the sin that we were about to commit caused a deep sickening feeling to rise in my throat.

"Keeya." The woman's voice startled me. It was my turn.

I looked at Caleb and got up slowly. In that moment, I wanted my baby more than anything. I began to cry. But, despite everything happening inside of me, I walked through that door to that room in the back. Frightened and fully aware that this was tragically wrong.

After the abortion, Caleb wouldn't answer my calls anymore. He was done with me for good. The abandonment of the relationship was too much for me to handle, so I reached out to Stacy for help. When I asked her to help me escape my troubled life, she didn't hesitate in doing her part to help me. After all, we were kindred spirits, both having been cast out by the Hall family. In a way, Stacy probably felt that she, too, was escaping her own hurts and pains vicariously by assisting me, a now-disillusioned sixteen-year-old.

So, decision made, she and I wheeled into the parking lot for the Greyhound bus station.

Reaching over, Stacy grabbed something from the glove compartment that piqued my curiosity, something that gleamed black. Aware the bus was leaving in fifteen minutes, though, I dismissed her action. I bolted from the rickety car, grabbing from the back seat everything I had in life: a backpack full of snacks, a notepad, favorite books I'd 'borrowed' from the library, the forest-green duffel bag from

Tony, and my most prized possession—my photo album.

We practically skip-walked through the parking lot, our enthusiasm inadvertently drawing the attention of some homeless men across the street from the bus station. One of the men raised his voice and blurted out a slurred obscenity. The others, encouraged, laughed and took turns making raspy cat calls. Instinctively, I clutched my belongings close to me. These men, from their garbled words, were obviously drunk even though it was only just noon.

Aware of the potential danger, Stacy stopped in her tracks and brandished what she had taken from the car for all to see: a small handgun. Empowered, she shouted back a few obscenities and threats of her own, words that left everyone dumbfounded.

Surprised, I looked at Stacy—and we burst into uncontrollable, nervous laughter. We crossed the remainder of the lot, the danger now behind us, and quickly reached the front door of the bus station.

With her smiling eyes, Stacy looked down at me and we embraced tightly. Never did I want to forget her kindness and protection.

When we parted, she reminded me, "Now, don't forget that you promised you would call me at every stop. I'm going to hold you to it!" Wiping my eyes, I agreed and forced a smile.

Satisfied, Stacy turned to leave, gun gripped tightly in her hand, and headed back to her car.

Once I saw she had left, I adjusted my belongings and opened the door to the station. Bucking up the courage, I walked straight to the ticket counter and purchased a ticket with the money I'd earned from working at a fast-food restaurant and the Eckerd drug store.

Ticket in hand, I wasted no time in heading for the Greyhound that waited outside. I was leaving Dallas, officially on my own, and making a new beginning for myself in Atlanta, Georgia. A fresh start. Who would have thought that $119 could purchase my freedom?

With each stop, a few passengers loaded or unloaded their belongings. At some stops, only one person would get on with a backpack. At others, an entire family might leave, allowing the remaining passengers to shuffle from seat to seat to get closer to the bathroom or to sit next to their travel buddy. I wondered what each of their stories was. Was anyone else running away from anything or anyone? Was I the only one trying to carve out a new life? I tried to make myself comfortable with my decision, but the more I tried to change my thoughts and to accept what I was doing, the more intense my mixed feelings became.

Eventually, sleep came to relieve my racing thoughts.

When I was awakened by the bus pulling into Birmingham, Alabama, my mind drifted to the times when our family moved from one city to another. I remembered the bewilderment of suddenly leaving behind the life that I'd become accustomed to and how Tony comforted me through the ongoing changes. I had always looked to him to make sense of it all. He had seemed to know how to calm my fears of being the new girl once again. The most sobering thought for me in this moment was that now there was no Tony around to calm the fear and restlessness that began to rise from that familiar place inside; the butterflies in my stomach darted and beat their wings relentlessly in angry and confused patterns. As he had said to me back then, I would have to learn to hug myself.

I admit I contemplated going to the ticket counter and in tears telling my story to a manager. I had wanted desperately for someone to know that I was alone in this world, that I only had about seventeen dollars to my name. I was terrified and I really wanted Mommy to kiss it and make it all better. I wanted someone to take me in and give me a place to sleep for the night, and then tell me I could live there and get my life together. Maybe they would tell me how to get my GED, and then I could enroll in college, make friends, and graduate like a normal person—and finally, I could have a normal life. Maybe.

That's all I really wanted. I wanted to live a life where I never moved unless it was within the city to a better place. And not frequently, but after, like, ten years or something. I wanted to live where people knew me and I knew them. I was tired of making new friends—it took too much time—when I knew I'd only have to start all over again. I was tired of packing and unpacking, of losing things in the move that were important to me.

At that moment, I remembered the stenographer's pad I'd left in Cincinnati. The one that, even after begging Daddy, I wasn't allowed to get. It was only a fifteen-minute walk from our house to Clifton Elementary. It would have taken less than five minutes to drive up the hill, park, and let me jump out and go to the office. They would surely have greeted me with a big hug and handed me my pad. By now, I could be reading all the comments my classmates had written, loving words that would bring me comfort and rescue me from this nothingness that felt like an abandoned cave in my heart right now.

A cave. Yeah, that's exactly what it felt like. I felt empty, forlorn. My thoughts became the stalagmite forming at the bottom of my dark, dampened heart. The tears that seemed to frequently drip from my eyes shaped into the most jagged salts, crystalized formations that wouldn't be discovered except by the lone animal—me—that would venture in to sleep on any given night. As far as I could see it, this was what life had become for me.

Then it hit me how Daddy was so selfish and mean. What kind of a father was he, anyway? Most men would want the best for their families and would jump at an opportunity to comfort their child, especially when the father was the reason that child had to move. Instead, he was awaiting trial for threatening my life and for beating Mommy. A trial that I, the chief witness, would never make.

In that moment, I changed my mind about turning around. What was I going back to? There was nothing to return to. And Tony wouldn't understand why I had to do this. I hadn't spoken to him in weeks at this point. The thought of going so long without speaking to him further ruined my mood.
What was done was done, and that was that.

My Ticket to Freedom?

It was night by the time I made it to Atlanta. At the station, I found the steps were steep and the pungent smells of oil, cigarette smoke, and exhaust reminded me of truck stops we had visited when traveling with Daddy. The sudden squeals of bus brakes made me jump. I stepped away from the Greyhound I'd exited and massaged my neck and shoulders, letting out a sigh. After the nineteen-hour ride, with stops in all the small towns along the way, I'd developed a nasty crick in my neck that no amount of stretching seemed capable of relieving.

As I stood around with other passengers waiting to claim my luggage, I stretched my legs. I looked around, trying to seem casual, like I rode the bus all the time and wasn't in a strange place waiting for an acquaintance to pick me up. I imagined the butterflies in my stomach were now flying like synchronized swimmers. I could picture them with their wings spread wide, one after the other diving into the acidic contents of my stomach. Despite this nervous fantasy, I was determined to prove to myself that I didn't need anybody but me to change things. Suddenly, the butterflies seemed to be upset with me for that thought; they were certainly in revolt for one reason or another. But no matter. I wasn't nervous or afraid or concerned—really. Instead, I pretended the flitting butterflies were private friends that symbolized the reality of my adventure taking on new meaning. It would have to be okay. It was *going* to be okay.

I had done this seemingly impossible thing—I had moved by myself from Dallas, Texas, to Atlanta, Georgia! Now, if only Todd would just hurry up and get here.

Once I spotted my familiar green bag, I grabbed it and headed into the bus station to look for my ride. Todd, at twenty-seven, carried himself like he was much older, so much that he reminded me more of Daddy's friends than anything. From what I recalled, he was about five nine, had a slightly big belly, and weighed close to one-hundred-and-eighty pounds. From the way he usually dressed, it was obvious that keeping up with the latest trends was not his forte.

His hair was slightly longer than when I'd seen him last, and I knew he was now sporting a beard instead of the usual goatee. I'd wondered about his morals since, knowing I was a minor, he didn't seem concerned about me coming to live with him. Still, I figured maybe our long talks had simply endeared me to him like a daughter or little sister.

Regardless, I certainly didn't want anything more than a platonic friendship. Besides, he wasn't my type in the least bit, anyway. I was into guys who were athletic and young, who wore trendy clothing or business attire with braided suspenders like Caleb did. Argh! I hated how every guy I met I compared to Caleb. Our relationship had died a terrible death, just like the child I'd briefly carried for him.

No, forget Caleb.

A sense of empowerment began to win the battle against the flock of angry butterflies within. Every decision was now mine to make, and there was absolutely no one to answer to. Yet as the thought of freedom became my companion, I realized that my ride was nowhere to be found. I squinted and scanned the crowd as the butterflies jostled inside. What if he forgot what time to pick me up? Or worse, what if he wasn't going to keep his promise to help after all?

As I tried to squelch the frantic feelings rising inside, a deep southern drawl suddenly greeted me from behind, causing me to nearly jump, "Hello, stranger!"

"Todd!" I whirled around, relieved. "I thought you'd forgotten all about me."

He looked at me with amazement and asked, "How could anyone ever forget you, Keeya?"

As we embraced, I jumped up and down in his arms like we were long-lost friends.

Honestly, I was more excited at the prospect of my freedom than to see him, but seeing him *was* my ticket to freedom, so I was even more glad to see him.

He gathered my things and we headed from the bus station to his car. As he loaded my belongings, I stood on the sidewalk, taking in the view of downtown Atlanta. I drew a deep breath and exhaled, happy to enjoy the fresh sight. I could just imagine the possibilities that were waiting for me in a place like this!

Then Todd approached me and put his hands around my waist, ruining the moment. I tensed up and placed my hands on his chest to push him away, feeling like I was trying to escape Pepe Le Pew of

Looney Tunes.

Todd, shocked at my response, withdrew and asked awkwardly, "Are you hungry? You had a long trip, and I know of a place that has amazing food. It's called Beautiful. It's a vegetarian restaurant and it's black-owned."

Frustrated, I backed off and replied, "Todd, that sounds nice, but can we just go through a drive-thru? I'm really tired."

"Sure, anything you want, Keeya. I'm just glad you're here."

I realized that I was angry at him. I knew that I had made it clear to him that we were just friends and that I just wanted a platonic relationship. I wondered how he could miss that fact when I had spent hours on the phone for almost a year, crying to him about the treatment I received from Daddy. I couldn't believe that he had just tried to pull that stunt of wrapping his arms around me like we were lovers. I needed to have a very serious talk with him. He needed to know that I wasn't in Atlanta for that.

And I just wanted to eat and sleep off this crick in my neck.

He took me to a small burger joint called Checkers. As we approached the menu at the drive-thru, Todd gave me a brief history of the restaurant's black owner, who became a millionaire through the chain. With this information, I felt a small confirmation of my decision to move here. I was impressed that the first and second places he offered to take me to eat were black-owned. If there were success stories like that here, maybe I *would* eventually make it big in Atlanta somehow.

But how?

We placed our orders and Todd paid for my food, though I fully intended to pay him back as soon as I got a job. The seventeen dollars and change I had was bus money needed for job searching next week.

As we pulled into a nicely manicured neighborhood, I admired the stucco houses and tall Georgia pine trees. I could see the red clay of the architecture even in the moonlight, which cast a glow on the driveway we slowly pulled into. We'd arrived at a nice one-story house with a beautiful yard, similarly styled like the homes we had passed yet it was certainly nothing like the apartment back home. I wondered how long it would take me to find work, save up my money, and have my own place. I doubted I could ever afford something like this.

As the host, Todd opened my door and grabbed my belongings, saying with a smirk on his bearded face, "Welcome to your new home."

When we made it to the front door, he said, "Keeya, don't worry. I'm going to take good care of you. There's nothing to be afraid of."

His words, however, had the reverse effect on me. I had never been more afraid and uncertain of a decision that I had made in my life! If he knew I just wanted to be friends, why was he speaking this way?

Despite my doubts, I followed him over the threshold—what else was I going to do? I certainly didn't have enough money for a hotel room. Tired from the journey, I asked where I would be sleeping. I assumed in a house this nice that the guest bedroom would be quaint and comfortable.

He hesitated and told me that the house was being remodeled and only the east wing was being used.

Though I couldn't see very much in the dimly lit, spacious house, I looked around and asked him again, "So, where am I sleeping?" He looked at me and said cheerfully, "In the master suite with me."

I was furious but tried not to show it. How could he pull such a trick? I felt like I had been conned. I pursed my lips and picked up my things. He offered to help but I refused.
He turned a hallway light on and guided me to his living quarters.

I looked at him and asked if he would respect my request and not expect me to 'give up the goods'. I reasoned with him about my need to decompress and just find a job and move on. But he didn't offer an alternative to the sleeping arrangement. I couldn't stand the fact that the rules to our agreement were changing. I could see from a mile away where this was headed. This must have been what Little Red Riding Hood felt when she was invited into her grandmother's house.

"Keeya, you can trust me," Todd promised me. "I won't do anything to hurt you. Just trust me, okay?"

His statements were neither believable nor reassuring. I knew now this wasn't going to be anything like I had planned. I knew what this could eventually lead to over time, and the more I looked at him, the more his wolf eyes seemed to gleam. There were holes in his story and I was going to get to the bottom of it all.
One lie only leads to another, Mommy always said that.

Todd showed me to the bathroom so that I could change into my night clothes. I set my suitcase and other bags down and searched for my sweatpants and a large t-shirt I'd stolen from Caleb—the most unappealing options I had. I would make every attempt to turn him off tonight. Once I found my way in the city, I'd leave here as quickly as I came.

By the time I'd changed, Todd was already in the king-size bed. He motioned for me to get in and I made it a point to lay between the comforter and the sheet, scooting to the edge. He got the message and left me alone for the night, and for this I was relieved.
My mind raced as I lay awake for hours in this unfamiliar bedroom.

Todd had fallen asleep a long time ago, and all I could hear was his slow breathing and the gentle hum of the ceiling fan.

Then I began thinking about what I had done. I pulled the t-shirt above the bridge of my nose to wipe the tears that raced down my cheeks and wet the sheets. I was terrified at my decision to leave Dallas. I longed to be in Caleb's arms again, but I knew that would never be a reality. He was the only man I'd ever loved and that relationship was over. I began to sob silently. With thoughts of Caleb clouding my mind, I pulled the covers tightly over my head and slowly drifted to sleep.

It was early Friday morning when I could hear the beautiful singing of the neighborhood birds. A smile emerged across my face as I realized that I had my new beginning, living arrangements aside. My money didn't match my goal of moving into my own place, but my plan was sure to work somehow. I had noticed last night there was a strip mall and various fast-food places within walking distance from the house—they seemed like good places to start.

My thoughts were interrupted by the sound of something crashing to the floor. I jumped up, throwing on a robe that was draped across the foot of the bed; with it, I noted there was a fresh towel, a face cloth, and a box of soap. Todd had a hospitable side after all.

I opened the bedroom door and rushed down the long hallway to the kitchen, where I saw Todd bending down to pick up pots that had fallen from a cabinet.

"Um, good morning, Todd. Can I help?" I asked cautiously.

"Oh, morning, Keeya. Nah, I'm just fine. Just wanted to surprise you with breakfast.

Looks like I still surprised you anyhow."

I thanked him for the bath supplies he had set out and told him I'd join him for breakfast after a shower.

I slowly headed back to the bedroom. As I went down the hallway, I couldn't help but notice the pictures that lined the walls. There were not many of Todd, except for a few baby pictures and one that was taken on a beach with a thin boy (who had to be Todd, because that was his unmistakable smile) and a shorter chubby boy.

There were several more recent pictures of two boys. You could tell by the high-top fades and the Karl Kani Cross Colours attire the boys wore. I searched for more photos of Todd, but there were none. Just more of another man and his wife and their two boys. It really nagged me.

I took my shower, taking care to lock the door behind me.

Todd served me a generous meal of hash browns, syrup-covered waffles sprinkled with cinnamon and powdered sugar, perfectly scrambled eggs, and linked sausages. I couldn't remember when I last had such a lavish breakfast! Afterward, we enjoyed a nice cup of coffee. There was even International Delight's French Vanilla coffee creamer!

Todd explained he had to get to work but that I was free to eat whatever was in the refrigerator. And since it was his pay day, he said he was going to show me another side of Atlanta after work—the nightlife! Since he had a friend working the door at the nightclub, there would be no problem getting me in.

At this news, a smug feeling came over me. Feeling quite like an adult, I smiled and sipped my coffee.

Although I wanted to go out and get a job ASAP, it seemed Todd wouldn't be able to take me job hunting until Monday. I had noticed an Eckerd drug store and a Wendy's, both of which I'd worked at before, so I was confident one of them would hire me if I applied. And if not, there was always the strip mall as backup.

In the meantime, I had clubbing to look forward to!

The Shock

As nine o'clock in the evening rolled around, Todd and I were almost ready for our night out. As he was in the other room, I heard him singing along with a song on the radio. He had a decent singing voice, and I thought to myself how he must have sung in the choir at church as a kid.

Something about the way he sang reminded me of Daddy singing in the bathroom of whichever home we occupied. Daddy's voice was way better. He was a trained singer who used to sing in the NCO clubs at the various bases where he was stationed. Mommy told me how he had sounded much better when he was young—before alcohol, cigarettes, and marijuana had taken their toll. Daddy was a true tenor and loved singing renditions of the Temptations, Stevie Wonder, Chuck Berry, and Marvin Gaye. He never sang entire songs, just the parts he liked. He often did this while shaving, and after he was finished, he would walk out of the bathroom with tiny white pieces of bathroom tissue stuck to his neck or chin by little red dots of blood.

I snapped out of my daydream about Daddy when Todd came out of the bathroom a changed man. He had on a black button-down dress shirt with a multicolored vest of geometric shapes, black dress pants that looked like they came from the cleaners , and two-toned black-and-brown Stacy Adams dress shoes.

I, on the other hand, looked like a cross between Janet Jackson and a backup dancer for Bell Biv DeVoe. I dyed my hair black, and I wore Mommy's red matte lipstick paired with a ton of mascara and black eyeliner. I wore a black scoop-necked bodysuit and Daisy Duke jean shorts with black opaque tights. A black baseball cap and black combat boots I'd picked up on sale from an Army-Navy store completed the look.

We arrived at the nightclub around ten o'clock. As we approached the entrance, Todd let me out while he found parking. I appreciated that he wanted to get me out of the house and have an enjoyable time, though I felt he seemed to have a few selfish motives up his sleeve. I was determined, however, to thwart his attempts of fulfilling any of them. I knew that getting a girl drunk to sleep with her was one of the oldest tricks in the book. After his sloppy stunts last night, my trust-o-meter was on high alert and I kept it pointed in his direction like a sniper in pursuit of her target.

Maybe he thought I'd forgotten about his advances, but his goals were at the front of my mind. I had every intention of wiggling away from him and finding my own fun and excitement tonight. I was encouraged by the steady thump of an intoxicating, familiar baseline coming from inside. It was one of my favorite songs: "Exclusivity" by Damien Dame.

I nodded my head to the beat, adjusted my satchel, pulled my cap low, and joined the line of partygoers. As far as anyone knew, I was a grown-up tonight. I laughed from the excitement of it all.

The line moved forward, and then I heard Todd call out to me. He came running and slid his arm around my waist. Irritated with his pseudo-possessive behavior, I was glad his action confirmed that losing him fast was my primary objective. I had already written his address on multiple pieces of paper to give to whoever I wanted to have it, but I first had to get inside and find someone else to have fun with.

"What's up, man? Long time," Todd said, greeting his friend at the door with a smirk. "Hey, man, this is Keeya. She's from Texas and is new to the city. Matter of fact, this is her second night here, and I wanted to take her out and show her a good time."
The grin on his face disgusted me, but I played along.

Noticing his friend was kind of hot, I extended my hand to shake his and flirted with my eyes. I put on the brightest smile that I could muster. "I'm sorry. Todd didn't bother to tell me your name."

The man grabbed my hand and kissed it just above the middle knuckle. "They call me Big D. Nice to finally meet you."
I tilted my head to the side and smiled, flattered.

Todd appeared shocked at the interaction between me and his friend, but Big D knew as well as I did that the joke was on Todd tonight.

We headed to the bar and Todd placed his order for a rum and Coke. I told the bartender to give me the same thing but to make it a double.

I was playing games with Todd, and I wish I could say that I hated myself for it, but I didn't. The look in his eyes was so intense, but I was smarter than Miss Red Riding Hood. The innocence in my face was my superpower. I knew exactly how to manipulate a man to get what I wanted. I was okay with being the carrot if it meant it would bring me closer to my goal. In the meantime, I danced a song with Todd to keep him chill for a while.

After a few more songs, we sat down near the bar. Todd ordered another round of rum and Cokes for us and I excused myself to go to the bathroom. Not because I needed to, but because across the room I spotted what Mommy would call a tall glass of water on a hot day! I had waited all night for this moment. I rushed through the crowd and began to slow my pace to pretend I didn't see Mr. Cool until I was directly in his line of vision. I put a little intensity in my walk like my friend, Carla, had shown me.

I knew how to walk down a runway from all the fashion shows that I participated in with Carla, who was like a big sister to me. She desired to become a professional model. She seemed to attract men unintentionally. They always appeared to have a lot of money or, at the very least, they valued time getting her attention. She was about five nine, with the complexion of Halle Berry and the body to go with it. She was a military brat like me, and she loved to introduce herself as an Amerasian because she was half-African American and half-Korean. She was only seventeen, but she knew how to get attention by the way she sashayed into a room. She would flash her smile and extend her hand slowly. There was certainly an art to the way she operated around men; I learned a lot more from her than I realized. If she had been here, we would have had so much fun cackling about this Todd guy.

Once I noticed the guy on the wall looking at me, I walked into his personal space and stopped. He had a gorgeous smile. He was about five eleven or so and had the build of a basketball player, noticeable through his white t-shirt, baggy stonewashed jeans, and black leather belt. Although he dressed simply, he could have been a model. I noted he also had black combat boots and all I could think was—*I'm legit!*

"Hi, there, I'm Keeya," I piped up, "and I'm new in town. Will you be here when I get back from the bathroom?" Even with a drink in me and the best smile on my face, I knew I sounded like a teenager.

"Sure, I'll wait for you," he said, taking a cool sip of his drink. He gave a wide smile that was almost a laugh, and then he adjusted his sunglasses, bobbing his head in sync to the music.

I entered the restroom and noticed an attendant selling squirts of perfume and sprays of deodorant. There were all kinds of things to buy: sticks of gum, bobby pins, safety pins, mints, and even condoms. I pulled out my red lipstick and reapplied it, not because I needed it, but because I didn't want to rush out of the bathroom too soon and appear eager.

Suddenly, two obviously drunk women burst into the bathroom laughing, neither of them able to stand up without wobbling over each other.

I remember thinking to myself how tacky they looked. In that moment, I decided that I didn't want to end up like that tonight. I briskly placed my lipstick back in my purse.

With a strong southern accent, the attendant asked me if I wanted anything, so I paid her for a squirt of White Diamonds perfume.

When I returned, the guy almost seemed to sense me coming and asked me to dance with him. He extended his hand and I followed him like a little puppy. I searched the club for Todd, but I couldn't see him through the massive pack of people. Well, whatever.

My favorite rap by Ice Cube came on, and everyone began to yell with excitement.

Obviously, I wasn't the only one who felt like it was their favorite.

The two of us danced hard. This guy had a ton of moves and he executed them like a pro.

I was having the time of my life, so I slipped him the address from one of the sheets I had prepared earlier. As I did so, I asked him for his name, having to yell over the thunderous music.

"They call me G-Man!" he replied.

When I asked him for his number, he nodded, but not before we danced to three more songs.

We left the dance floor, moist with perspiration, and went to the bar. While I asked for a rum and Coke, he began to write his number down on a napkin, which I tucked away. Satisfied with my accomplishment, I downed my drink a bit too fast and had to take a few deep breaths to keep everything at bay. I then glanced over at G-Man's drink, which was bluish green.

"What is that? Can I taste it?" I said a little too quickly. G-Man answered, "Midori Sour."

I tried to act composed, but the deep tone of his voice in that moment captivated me completely. That's when I knew I was in trouble. My curiosity was at its peak and I was certainly tipsy.

Suddenly, I heard a voice behind me ask tightly, "Can I have this dance?" It was Todd, who was clearly annoyed.

Oh, right. He was still here.

I turned around to him and said, "I'll be with you in just a second, okay? I'll come and find you."

Todd shook his head and walked off.

I turned back around and looked at G-Man, who was sipping his drink with his eyebrows raised.

He asked, "What was that all about?"

"Oh, nothing really. That was my uncle, who I came with. He's so overprotective that I'm not allowed to have fun without him breathing down my neck."

I left G-Man to look for Todd, who was in a corner by himself. "What was that about, Todd?" I asked.

"What was that about, Keeya?" he fired back.

"Listen, Todd, I appreciate you bringing me out tonight, but you don't own me," I said, not caring to mask my aggravation.

"Keeya, I'm not trying to own you, but I came to the club with you and I'm spending my money to make sure you have a good time—and you're spending it with someone else."

"Well, consider that I just saved you some money because that guy bought me a couple of drinks that you didn't have to pay for." I could feel myself becoming more and more angry. The nerve of him trying to tell me how I can or cannot enjoy my night!

"Keeya, I'm not going to lie. I find you very attractive and I know your situation.

Tonight, I just wanted to have fun and not think about problems or anything like that. I wanted to spend this time with you, show you around, you know? After all, you did come to live with me."

He had a point with that last statement, but I wasn't going to let him know that I agreed with him. I rolled my eyes and crossed my arms in protest. I knew I was being a spoiled brat, but at the heart of the matter, I was not attracted to Todd like he was to me.

Feeling we needed to clear the air, I asked him. "Todd, do you want to be more than friends?"

He looked uncertain and hesitated. I could tell that he didn't want to upset me, so he chose his words carefully. "Keeya, since I met you on that flight to Tulsa, I knew you were a special person. I know that you aren't attracted to me. I'm just some lame older guy to you. But this isn't the best environment to talk about this. I think it's time we leave."

"Yeah, let's do that," I answered, secretly relieved to be out of there.

On the way back to his place, we didn't talk for a while. I chose to look out the window and admire the night sights of the city.

Todd, who had been deep in thought, finally said, "Keeya, there is something that I need to talk to you about."

This got my attention, so I glanced over at him and asked, "What is it?"

He took a deep breath. "I wasn't completely honest with you about my house. It's actually my brother's house…and I'm just house-sitting."

My jaw dropped.

He continued, "I feel really bad, but something happened on his recent trip—his son became ill, so they'll be back sooner than expected."

"So, when were you going to tell me about this, Todd?" I exclaimed, fuming.

He answered quickly, "I planned on telling you this week. I had a plan to move into my own apartment, but it fell through. I've already been accepted to another place, but my brother is coming into town tomorrow and he doesn't want you staying at the house. Says he has too much to sort out and doesn't feel all that hospitable right now. I'm really sorry, Keeya. I can pay for your ticket back home, and when I move into my apartment, you can come stay with me."

At Todd's news, I no longer felt tipsy. My night came in for a crash landing. My thoughts began to race as if they were competing for the Indy 500 trophy.

I said out loud, "I can't believe this is happening to me. Todd, this isn't cool at all. I don't have anywhere to return to. How could you leave out such an important detail? You flat-out lied to me about the house, and now you want me to believe that you'll send for me when you get settled? Who says I trust you after telling me this?"

His voice changed, like he was aware he was obviously in the wrong. "Keeya, I wanted to help you when you told me what you were up against with your father. I wasn't thinking this through. Like I said, I had an apartment that fell through. I was planning to move in next week. I-I thought you would understand."

I tuned him out. I thought about the family pictures I had passed in that hallway—the family was his brother's. I thought about how nice the furniture was and how his call center job couldn't have afforded it. My mind switched to thinking about how I was going to go home, who I might live with. Certainly not Mommy. Daddy would be home any day, and I didn't want to suffer retaliation for having the cops send him to jail because of my absence. I had a strained relationship with Tony's wife, Kendall, so I couldn't stand the idea of asking for their help.

My mind drifted to the day Kendall physically fought me and Mommy. She came with Tony to confront Mommy about how I was being raised. He, for example, didn't like how I was homeschooled. It didn't matter that I went to City Hall meetings every Wednesday or that I was the youngest member of Recycling Minority Business Dollars in Dallas and had that small business selling aquariums. I was getting real-world experience, but it was all hogwash to him. In his opinion, I was being robbed of a childhood, I guess. He also knew that Mommy was so depressed on most days that, rather than check my assignments, she would just sleep. At one point, my assignments were backed up for over a month; Mommy merely went through them and pencil whipped my grades. Kendall believed I would get better care at a home for juvenile delinquents.

The day they arrived, I heard a bunch of commotion at the front door and realized they were all in each other's faces, yelling and screaming, Mommy against Tony and Kendall. I was angry seeing the two of them disrespect Mommy, after all she had done for us. Although it was painful to hear Mommy belittle them (I knew she was capable of better), I couldn't stand to see this take place. I jumped in and yelled at them to stop.

The next thing I knew, Mommy had spit in Kendall's face. In the tense silence that followed, I told them to leave. For a moment, no one moved. Then Kendall reared back and punched Mommy in the face.

Filled with fury, I jumped on Kendall and we fought, my one-hundred-and-fifteen pounds against her two-hundred-and-fifty pounds. Tony tried to break it up but was unsuccessful. We were like alley cats, shrieking at each other. Vaguely, I was aware that people were coming out of their apartments to see what was happening. We tussled out of the apartment, down the steps, and across toward the pool and the game room. What was mere seconds seemed to go on forever.

Finally, Mommy stopped yelling and cut in to take a swing at Kendall and they physically locked arms. As they fell to the ground, Kendall got the best of Mommy.

Tony intervened, yelling, "Release her, Kendall. This has gone too far.

Release her!"

It looked like Mommy was about to get kneed in the head when a tall man yelled from the balcony, "Kendall, let her go—it's not worth it."

Mommy, released, gasped for air. As she slowly got up, she spat to Tony, "I never want to see either of you again. Don't so much as come this way to these apartments. Tony, you've made your choice. Kendall's all yours, but you've lost me forever."

Such severed ties. This memory made me upset, and I felt sick at the thought of going 'home'. *What home?* I thought. *Go back to what? Tony—and his wife, who I despised—or to Mommy, who I left in a townhouse that my three part-time jobs halfway paid for? So, what? That Daddy can come home from jail and make good on his promise to kill me?*

"Unbelievable." I didn't mean to say it out loud, but I couldn't help it.

Todd pulled into the driveway. We entered the house without speaking a word to each other.

I gathered my belongings from his room and used the hallway bathroom to wash up for the night. I'd never actually entered this bathroom before. I could see how it was decorated for children. Everything Todd had said in the car began to sink in. Ugh! If he could have just told me the truth from the beginning, I would have waited to come.

That night, I chose to sleep on the sofa.

Upon waking up the next day, I felt a knot in the pit of my stomach. The kitchen clock read 11:45 a.m., and as much as I tried to go back to sleep, my racing mind refused to let me.

My thoughts were interrupted by the sound of a vehicle pulling up in the driveway. I jumped up to see who it was through a window: it was a Super Shuttle. The side door opened and a stocky black passenger jumped out. He went to the back of the van, and the driver jumped down to help him get his luggage.

Uh-oh.

Hastily, I gathered my things and ran into Todd's bedroom.

"He's here!" I whispered as I shook Todd vigorously. "Get up, it's your brother!" "Kev—oh, shoot!" Todd scrambled to his feet and threw on his robe. "I forgot to pick
him up from the airport. He's going to be so pissed."

As I grabbed my toiletries, I heard the front door open and the sounds of entering footsteps. I ran into the hallway bathroom and closed the door behind me. Flustered, I turned on the faucet to begin brushing my teeth, trying to act normal. I could overhear the two men talking, but their voices were too muffled to make out what was being said. I quickly resorted to my investigative tactic, learned from our landlady in

Cincinnati, who was humorously known for eavesdropping by placing a glass against the door to amplify the conversation in the other room.

All I had was a paper Dixie cup, but that didn't work too well. I slowly opened the door to hear better.

Todd was exclaiming, "This is temporary until I move in on the fifth. Why are you always so negative, man?"

"If you think that's harsh," his brother shot back, "just let her be here when Janice gets here. You ain't heard nothin' yet. If you weren't so prone to lying about everything, I could try to help. But your lies have gotten me in trouble for the last time. The thing I'm tryin' to get you to see is that harboring a minor is illegal, bro! Why don't you think? I've got enough to deal with rather than add this to my list of worries. When you get your own place, you do what you want to do. But in here, I call the shots. If you don't tell her, I will and that's a fact."

It was official. My Plan A was a fail.

I wanted to go hide under a rock. After hearing that conversation, I had no desire to meet Kevin or his wife. I was embarrassed and even more angry that Todd had not been honest with me.

I had to think quickly. I didn't want to be here any longer than necessary. If I had to live on the streets, I was going to. Anything but moving back to Dallas. I decided to do the only thing that I could. After all, I was essentially being kicked out, so I had nothing to lose at this point. I took my shower and got dressed as quickly as possible. With my suitcase, I went to the kitchen, where Todd was pouring a cup of coffee.

"Todd," I firmly admitted, "I heard an earful earlier. I just want to know if there is a quiet place where I can use the phone. I really need some privacy to make some arrangements."

"Sure, Keeya," he said, defeated. "Use the phone in the guest room." He pointed down toward another hallway.

"Guest room? I thought that side of the house was being remodeled."

"If you want to use the phone, that's where it is. The first door to the left."

All I could think of was how his lies were catching up with him at an alarming rate. I said nothing as I walked through the part of the house that was 'being remodeled'.

Such a liar. I thought to myself. I was increasingly angry at myself for taking him at his word. I should have trusted my gut.

I entered the guest room, which was sparsely decorated with a full-size bed and a small table with a lamp. There was a small TV on a table in the corner and an unassuming bookcase.

I unfolded the napkin with G-Man's number written on it and used the rotary dial telephone to input the digits. I was amused by this ancient phone, which reminded me of the phones in Grandma's apartment.

A man's voice answered.

I hesitated and asked the question, "Yes, can I speak to G-Man?" The man replied, "Sure, can I tell him who's calling?"

"Yes, tell him it's Keeya."

I heard the man yell in the background, "Aye, G, pick up the phone!"

I was so nervous doing this. But I had come this far, and since turning around and going back was not an option, neither was being timid. I had absolutely nothing to lose.

"Hello, Keeya."

"Hi, G-Man. I didn't wake you or anything, did I?"

"Nah, I've been up washing my car. How did everything go with your uncle last night?" "Not too great. That's what I was calling to talk to you about."

At this point, I knew I would have to lie to make my story what I needed it to be. I wasn't ready to tell him about Daddy, so I was going to have to make this all about my 'uncle'.

"G-Man, I have to be honest with you. I know you don't really know me, but I need a place to stay tonight because my uncle is mad at me about a lot of things. He feels that I don't respect him. He was angry that I was dancing with you, but he's just being unreasonable. I moved here from Dallas to go to school. He's my only family here, but he cussed me out so bad just now and told me to pack up my things and leave. It's…it's really messed up. It's crazy, I know, but my dorm will be ready in August, so it won't be for long. I just need to get a job and get my stuff situated."

"How old are you, if you don't mind me asking?" he inquired.
"Eighteen," I said confidently. Another lie.
"Wait, how'd you get in the club?" "My uncle knew the guy at the door." "I see."

"How old are you, G-Man?"

"I'm twenty-two. Just had a birthday last week. Me and my brother were celebrating it last night."

"I feel stupid asking a stranger for a place to stay," I confessed. "You must think I'm crazy or something."
"No, I get how family can be. The same thing almost happened to me last year with Pops.
We got into it because I called him out on his drinking, and he bit my head off. I came to live with my brother and never looked back. We're good people. I'll see what I can do. Can you give me about a half hour or so to discuss the situation with my brother, and then you can call me back, okay?"

I gave him forty-five minutes for good measure, which felt like hours. It is never a simple decision to let someone come and live with you. Something inside of me wanted to pray, but I was afraid that God wouldn't want to be involved in this level of chaos. Plus, I had lied, so surely that prayer wasn't going to work for me now.

Knowing the rotary would only go so fast, I took my time dialing the phone number. The whirring sound it made distracted me until I heard G-Man come on the line.

"Hello?" he said.

"Hi, there, it's Keeya," I ventured uneasily.

"Can you be completely ready by six? I have to run a few errands before coming for you."

"Yes, I'll be ready!" I exclaimed. "Oh, G-Man, thank you so much!"

"You're welcome," he replied affably. "Just one thing. I have some friends that I need to talk to about helping you out. They have a bigger space than we do, but you can spend the night here. We'll get this all figured out."

"Wow. I don't know how to thank you. You have no idea!" I gave him the address and hung up the phone. My plan had changed and I was both relieved and afraid.

Now, I was going to a complete stranger's house. Was I nuts?

In Too Deep

The most confusing excitement came over me as the truth sank in that I was going to live with strangers. It was dangerous, but something about it was fun. This was turning out to be quite the adventure, and I was pleased that I had overcome my current predicament all by myself.

It didn't take long for me to pack my things. Realizing that I had a few hours before

G-Man came, I rested on the sofa, aware Todd was quietly observing me. Miffed at him, I had decided not to tell him my plans. I wasn't even going to say I was leaving until the very last minute. As far as I was concerned, what I did wasn't his business.

Six o'clock finally crawled up and I found I couldn't stop looking out the window, which piqued Todd's attention.

"Are you waiting on someone?" he asked in a concerned tone. "Yes, a friend is picking me up," I said crisply.

"A friend? You mean the guy you met at the club—and you think I didn't see the exchange?"

"Yes," I admitted, "and that isn't your business."

"Huh." He crossed his arms. "You might be making a mistake."

"Yeah, well, I'll take my chances. But I really don't think you need to worry. He's taking me to the bus station." Another lie. I didn't want Todd's judgment or his advice. He had screwed up big time with me and I was just ready to leave his brother's house and never speak to him again.

We were interrupted by the sound of a car pulling up.

I rushed to the front door and opened it, waving at G-Man, who was seated in a shiny black Monte Carlo SS. I hurried back to gather my things, which Todd was holding for me.

"Thanks," I said, taking my bags, "I'll call when I get back home."

Well, I had to say something. Although he didn't know it, that call would never come.

I ran out to the car, where G-Man popped the trunk and put my bags inside. As I slipped in the passenger side, G-Man flashed me his million-dollar dimpled smile.

"Hey, you," he said.

"Hey, yourself!" I replied, excited.

"Well, we'll be on our way. We live about forty-five minutes away, so sit back and relax.

Oh, and I hope you don't mind the jazz I'm playing. It relaxes me. I figured you need some of that in your life."

"Wow, how'd you know?"

With the low-key music thrumming in the background, we slowly pulled out of the driveway. I glanced back at the house and saw Todd standing in the window, watching us. I couldn't read his expression, but I didn't care.

Good riddance to that liar! I thought, and turned my attention to the scenery, secretly hoping I'd never see it again.

As we headed down various streets, my thoughts returned to the fact that I had just entrusted my safety and life into the hands of someone I hadn't even known for twenty-four hours yet. Now boxed in by an intimidating uncertainty, I felt like I was making a mistake. But I had to start somewhere, right? Somehow, I had to survive.

A while later, G-Man fiddled with the radio and landed on V-103. The host, Ryan Cameron, came on the air and joked about the condom fashion accessory TLC's Left Eye wore before playing the R&B group's hit song, "Ain't 2 Proud 2 Beg". I nodded to the beat before I noticed G-Man regarding me thoughtfully.

"What do you think about being in a music video?" he asked.

"A music video? I think it would be cool. What made you ask that?"

"Well, I have a few connections with some music producers, including the one who did this song. He's a young cat and if he likes you, you're in. It's that simple."

I stared at him, my eyebrows raised. "Wow, can I get paid for being in it?"

"That all depends on the label. It's not my decision, but I can make the introduction. Just keep your cool around everybody. He's a cat with some clout. It's not a thing you want to mess up."

"Oh, I know how to act," I reassured him.

Well, I knew a little about music producing. After all, Tony used to make beats to raps for his friends all the time when we lived in Tulsa. Most of them, made for Tony's own enjoyment, were Christian raps (if our parents heard anything else, he would surely have to give up his equipment). I don't know if he ever got paid for his work, though. If he did, it wasn't that much.

One Saturday afternoon, I remember hearing Tony rapping to a beat. I had just come out of the bathroom and happened to see his door cracked. He was so into it that he didn't notice me walk in and sit on the edge of his bed. He rhymed:

Eve was slowly walkin' through the garden one day When Satan the snake said, 'Baby, come my way,
I have a few things that I want to say.

Did you know that you can eat from the big, bad tree? It'll make you like God, it'll set you free.
Go ahead, baby, give it a try,

'Cause when you're just like God, you cannot die—'

"Go, Tony!" I interrupted.

"Oh, hey, Keeya. You like my new beat?" "Yeah, that's pretty good, Tony."

I really missed him. I wished things were like when we were younger. Before he got married and all.

So, where could I go from here? Could I make something of myself if things went well with this music producer? Maybe I'd mix with big names and experience a small slice of the celebrity life, or I'd be a part of the up-and-coming groups who were seeking to make it big in the competitive music industry. Atlanta was full of singers, rappers, musicians, and producers. I'd surely carve out my niche somewhere.

Eventually, we arrived at G-Man's apartment complex, a heavily wooded and somewhat secluded area. The sun was completely buried beneath the deep, blue-black sky. As we got out of the car, G-Man grabbed my things and I followed him to a brick-red door. All I could think of was how crazy everything was unfolding. I hadn't been in town for a week and now I was in a complete stranger's home. Once we were inside his apartment, I could see it was certainly a bachelor's pad. The furniture was nice, eclectic like G-Man's tastes, but it needed a woman's touch.

G-Man waved his hand in front of my face, jolting me out of my observations. "Helloooo. I was saying, 'Welcome to my and my brother's abode.' You'll probably be here just for a day or two. I think I have a place for you to live for a while. As it turns out, I'm hardly here, so I think it would be better for you."

"Where's the other place, and who would I be living with?" I figured he had some family or female friends that he'd been speaking to about me.

"As crazy as it seems, the producer I was telling you about just put two of his groups in an extended-stay hotel until their next place is ready."

"Okaaaay." And that meant…?

"So, we're gonna roll by there tomorrow night and if you think you can hang, you'll have a place to lay low and get yourself together."

"What can you tell me about these people?" Knowing I was going to be living with people I wasn't even acquainted with, I couldn't help but wonder what in the heck I was getting myself into.

"These are young black guys who party a lot. One of the groups is a bunch of rappers, and the other is my boss's own singing group. It may be shocking, but these are decent people just trying to make it like everybody else. We're kinda like a family. We take care of each other. You cool with it?"

"I don't really have a choice right now," I managed to answer. My stomach was developing knots. This was getting potentially scary.

"I think you need to meet them and then you can see for yourself. You can put your things in the hallway closet, and the sofa is comfortable when you're ready to turn in."

"Okey-dokey," I replied, trying to sound carefree. "I'll bring you some covers and a pillow."

"Sounds good to me. Listen, uh, thanks for helping me out here.

My mind is a bit chaotic right now."

He smiled. "Wait right here—I know what will help you to relax." He hurried off. If he had something for me to relax, then I was all for it.

Soon, G-Man came back with a purple drawstring bag that had gold lettering and a couple of glasses filled with ice. Opening the bag, he pulled out a bottle of Crown Royal whiskey.
We sipped and talked for hours it seemed. We laughed about everything.

With the night having passed with no incidents, the next morning was a bit awkward, to say the least. We ate breakfast, and then I watched TV all day in between naps and even cleaned the kitchen while G-Man went to run some errands.

When I was by myself in the empty apartment, though, I found I already regretted my decision. It wasn't really clear what would happen next. Sure, I'd briefly entertained grandiose ideas of achieving stardom, but now my reality looked uncertain. I wondered how Mommy was doing. I had told her I was leaving, but she'd freak out if she knew how I was behaving and who I was with. Heck, *I* was freaking out! I had given Todd such a hard time, but I was repulsed by him and his advances. G-Man, in contrast, was so chill about everything. He just seemed easier to trust.

When G-Man returned, he was happy and singing to himself (he wasn't much of a singer, though, that's for sure). As I watched him pick up around the house, I decided to jump in the shower. Afterward, I overheard him on the phone.

"Yeah," he was saying, "Shorty's legit. She's real cool, man. Just give us a few, and we'll be over. All right, man, see you soon."

I was kinda nervous about meeting the groups. This adventure was getting crazier by the minute. I came out after getting changed and saw G-Man, who was eating an apple in the living room.

"Hey, there. What's going on?" I asked.

"Yeah, I just got off the phone with Denver, the lead of the rap group I told you about." "Really? Are we going over there?"

"Yeah, we're going over there. And Dustin is passing through with Reggie later on. They want to meet you."

"They do?"

"Yeah, I told them you might want to be in their upcoming video when they shoot it,

too."

"Okay, cool. So, they know I need a place to stay?"

"Yeah, I told them you needed a place until your dorm was ready."

Right, the school story. "Okay," I answered. "Well, let's do it. Let's meet them." "We'll run to Greenbriar Mall first so I can pick up a few things, then we'll swing
through there."

"Anything you say, G-Man." I decided I was down for whatever. I had nothing to lose.

After the small errand, we pulled up to the extended-stay hotel, Executive Suites, that was for business travelers—but I saw more people there who didn't resemble business travelers at all. I was a bit tired from riding around with G-Man, so I stretched my legs before I followed him up the steps. I couldn't help feeling like a little kid as I tagged along. As we approached, I could smell one of the most familiar scents—it reminded me of how Daddy smelled on the weekends.

G-Man knocked on the door and a tall guy in a white shirt greeted us with a big smile on his face.

"Well, ain't you gonna introduce us?" the man asked, before stepping out and circling me. "And what do we have here?" He smiled between drags on his Newport cigarette.

G-Man walked me in and the rest of the guys in the room glanced at our entrance. G-Man announced, "Here she is, everybody. This is Miss Keeya."

Everyone stood up and politely introduced themselves before sitting back down and returning to their activities.

I inhaled that familiar scent deeply—and then I spotted the joint being passed around. I had never used drugs. I was just used to smelling it on Daddy sometimes when he would come home. Mommy always argued about how he smelled, and he would just laugh uncontrollably. I never understood it.

For a moment, I just stood there, a bit overwhelmed by the new environment. I knew that I was in too deep, but I couldn't leave right then and there. I scanned the room for a place to sit when suddenly a voice in the dining area said, "Have a seat, girl. We don't bite."

I looked up to see who was talking and saw it was a guy of my complexion. He was kind of short and sported a blond afro. He looked like he had eyeliner on, which made his eyes look piercing.

"Okay," I said as I took my seat next to the TV.

G-Man came over and pulled up a chair next to me, joint in hand. He asked, offering, "Do you smoke?"

"Smoke? I never have," I admitted, feeling naïve. "Do you want to try it?"

I was nervous, but I was also curious and I couldn't think of a reason not to. "Sure, I'll try it."

"Are you sure? I don't want you to feel like you have to."

I dismissed his words. I didn't want to seem like a little girl. I wanted to appear tough in this room full of men, so I put the joint to my lips and pulled a lot, inhaling deeply, quickly—and began coughing uncontrollably.

Laughing, G-Man slapped my back, and someone quickly brought me a glass of water.

Already, I was feeling lightheaded and a bit dizzy. I began to laugh a bit. It was a different laugh, though. Nervous and shocked. The more I thought about it, the more I laughed. I felt so silly all of a sudden. This must have been what Daddy had been going through. Now I could see where he was coming from.

Then I noticed a deck of cards on a nearby table and I asked if anyone knew how to play Spades. The room lit up at my question.
The guy in the dining area quipped, "You know how to play?" "Yeah," I said. "I got some skills."

The next thing I knew, we were at the table and I was being dealt my hand; inside, I grinned at their acceptance. You would have thought I was one of the boys.

Over the course of the night, I felt like everyone kept interviewing me. I, in turn, interviewed them back. I was actually having what I thought was the time of my life. Then I heard someone at the door and four guys walked in.
G-Man quickly came to me, motioning me to join him. "I want you to meet someone."

I rightly guessed it was the producer, Dustin. He had on a black leather jacket decorated with various colors. Underneath, he wore a white t-shirt and light blue jeans. When I walked over, I could tell he was sizing me up with a smile on his face.
Wanting to make a good first impression, I smiled my brightest smile. "Hi, I'm Keeya.

It's nice to meet you, baby. You just met a millionaire!"

He merely laughed, while his companions were startled and amused.

I have to admit I found him charming. I had tried to act normal yet memorable and I had succeeded. G-Man thought I'd done well. I would come to observe, in the days and weeks ahead, that as quickly as Dustin made his entrance, he would just as quickly slip out. He might stay and take a few drinks, smoke a joint, and then leave. He was always checking on the groups to see how everyone was doing.

G-Man wanted to know how I was doing at the end of the night. I was incredibly tired, but I told him I was fine. The last thing I remembered was falling asleep on the couch with a drink in my hand.

This became my home for about six or seven months. I was the only girl between the two groups, which totaled twelve guys. Dustin, his older brother, Clyde, and Derrick, who seemed to be his right-hand man, would come through occasionally and kick it. The wild parties continued, and each time I pushed the limits further and further.

It wasn't long before even more unspeakable things happened as I was quickly caught up in the celebrity lifestyle. So easily was I sucked into the entertainers' lowest pastimes ad nauseum.

Under the Radar

There were a few times when I was allowed to go to whatever show the groups were a part of to help with promotions. Sometimes, we would load up in Clyde's black Isuzu Trooper or Denver's white two-seater Mercedes. Even Dustin would pull up in his white Jeep Wrangler, the one with the bedazzled wheel covers of one of the celebrity groups he managed. I was impressed by the flashy vehicles. Never would I have seen anything like these back at home.

Sometimes, girls from the local universities would tag along and they would wonder who I was. When I would tell them that I lived with two of the groups Dustin was producing, they would have puzzled expressions on their faces.

I even remember meeting and partying with one congressman's daughter, Cookie, who had the most adorable Volkswagen Rabbit that I had ever seen. Oh, how I wanted to be her: the daughter of a notable politician, a girl who went to the best schools. She was so nice and respectable in my book. I wanted to reach out and ask for her help, but I had no idea where to start. Instead, when I would see her, we would exchange small talk and she would be on her way. What did I think she could do? We were from two very different worlds. I wondered what she thought of me. Did she ever think about how every time she came to visit, I was there, morning, noon, and night?

One of the greatest difficulties for me was finding the next place to live, to remain under the radar as a minor. To be picked up by a truancy officer would have been a nightmare since I lived in a different city from my parents. Would they extradite me back to Texas? I couldn't take any chances, so I ventured out at night only, checking out which places were available. I was not old enough to sign a lease and neither did I have a job or a car in order to be gainfully employed.

Therefore, I decided to do the next best thing. Since I was familiar with nightclubs, I entered a miniskirt contest at the local Diamonds and Pearls. This is where I discovered my 'talent' of dancing. I say that with huge amounts of sarcasm, though, because the form of dancing I employed was not artful nor genuinely praise-worthy; instead, it resulted in the most degrading attention I had ever publicly experienced up to that point. Because I was a part of Dustin's entourage, I was never carded. And when I came in first place in my first miniskirt contest, I won a year-long VIP membership, not to mention a much-appreciated stash of prize money.

I loved the attention that I received at the club when the crew was there. They treated me like a celebrity. I rarely paid for drinks, for example, because one of the staff would remember me from a contest or someone in the VIP area would offer me one.

I was the undisputed miniskirt champion for a few months until some girl who worked at Magic City came. I guess she had a lot of customers who knew her very well. I couldn't compete. Man, those Magic City girls were professionals. She did things on the dance floor that made even me blush.

Honestly, I desperately wish that I could unsee many of the

things that I witnessed there—the provocative dances, the drunken men encouraging us on, the money fanned out before me. My innocence was so far removed from me that I would search my face in the mirror, straining to see the wide-eyed, enthusiastic girl from months ago (Or had it been years?).

One day, I was in the bathroom at the groups' hangout, peering in the mirror, trying to find her. Where was she? The former me, the one who played in the park near our house in Ohio, chasing yellow butterflies that pretended to play with me for what seemed like hours. Where was the little girl who allowed her finger to be the bridge that the ladybug used to crawl across from the edge of one leaf to another in the springtime? Where was the little girl who, after a storm, stooped down to discover a lone worm struggling against the ridges of the concrete. Each ring of this shiny brownish creature contracted like an accordion being played by a skilled musician.
When I moved in closer to help this poor creature get across the sidewalk to the dewy grass, the edge of my sandal accidentally trapped half of its body beneath. I lifted what I could see of the poor creature and saw it had become two wiggly pieces, torn asunder by my curiosity and my sandal. Part of its terrible insides squirted into my eye, causing me to cry. I decided that day those icky worms and I could never forgive each other for what had just transpired. We were officially enemies.

As I searched my heart for other memories that could somehow redeem me from my current reality, the door opened and Dustin entered to let me know that Derrick had brought groceries that I should go and put up before they began to spoil. Then the guys were gone, leaving me,

Cinderella, to do the chores.

This was a normal day for me. The culmination of everything I did, day in and day out, was never followed by a sense of accomplishment or privilege, but that of shame and hopelessness.

I found my relationship with the guys confusing, dissonant. Some days, we got along like I was their little sister. I was accepted as part of the family. They looked out for me and were even protective of me to an extent. As a result, I suffered greatly from a form of Stockholm Syndrome. No one could say anything bad about them to my face. After all, they'd taken me in when I had nowhere else to go. They had my back.

But did they really?

When nights came and it was time to party, my role of kid sister quickly changed. It was a silent understanding that in order to live there and hang out with them, I had to be available to 'benefit those in need'. No one felt the need to ask my permission, but I didn't refuse them very much either. But who were they that I was so insignificant to them? Did they really have no qualms about the very mixed messages they were sending me? Didn't they have sisters or mothers who taught them how to treat people?

Why, in these moments, was there no one to wipe the tears from my face and comfort me? Each time I cried over my situation, I felt my heart tighten and another layer of bitterness form and slowly crystalize over the throbbing ache inside. Oh, how I longed to be truly valued and esteemed. But it would never happen here. I was no more significant than the maids who came in to change the linens and bring more towels.

Yeah, I appeared in videos, I ate at wonderful restaurants, I met celebrities, and I went shopping at Phipps Plaza and Lenox Square—but the cost was too great!

It was such a mixed-up, disturbing world to me. I remember when we would all go to Stone Mountain to see Dustin's family, and there were kids around and his model girlfriend, Kay, who was the most beautiful black woman I'd ever seen. She had the cutest toddler, who was from a previous relationship with a famous R&B singer. Dustin's mother, though, was my favorite. Everyone called her Ma-bell, and she was known to cook like an angel. But what always stunned me was the way everyone lived and interacted. It all appeared so...normal on the surface. Like there was nothing shady going on. Occasionally, someone would ask me why I was always with the guys and I would say I was a backup dancer. It was a half-truth because I *did* dance onstage at a show at Center Stage and I *was* in two of the group's music videos. I would never admit to anyone my real role.

I even remember at Christmas when the guys formed a huddle at the hotel one afternoon and Dustin presented me with a round trip plane ticket to visit Mommy. I was so grateful for their gift, but I was very afraid to see her. I couldn't possibly tell her what her baby girl had really been up to. We barely spoke on the phone. But, oh, how I missed her! It made me think deeply about what I was really doing. I was in denial that I was a bad person. I was surviving, I was living, and, at times, I was happy. Right?

The sad truth of my life was that I was just a live-in groupie who was brought to industry parties for the 'after party'. I was a secret, a worthless nobody. I was under the radar and no one knew about it. I was a mess, I was trapped, and I knew I needed out.

Since I had lied about my age, though, I didn't want to be put out to look for another place. Of all of the places I'd looked up, I found that my current lifestyle as music groupie and miniskirt girl actually provided a dependable pattern—there was always a place I could crash and a degree of financial security available to me. The Stockholm Syndrome I suffered often twisted my thinking so that I believed these people were my family and that our relationships were somehow okay and that it was a consensual living arrangement. In my gut, though, I knew I was delusional. When it came down to it, I could have sued Dustin and settled out of court for some real big money. But, no, I preferred to quietly pretend I was living a normal life. And I wore my private shame like a glitzy badge every time I escorted them in public.

And in spite of all this foolishness I was engaged in, I had a huge crush on Dustin, even though I'm pretty sure he would deny even knowing a minor if he was ever asked. I often fantasized about him, that the lavish and sensual experiences I had were between me and him alone.

I wanted to be his love interest like his model girlfriend and not an infrequent pit stop where someone was always looking on as I changed his tires. I imagined that he would pick me up one day and look deeply into my eyes and promise to take me away from all this madness. I envisioned us riding in his black Range Rover, the sun peeking through the Atlanta skyline while sleek shadows moved across his leather dashboard and we listened to one of the latest groups that he was producing. He would glance at me and offer a coy but masculine smile. I would lean across the armrest and brush my lips against his face, just beneath his ear, and inhale his cologne with satisfaction.

We would pull up to his high-rise condo located across from Phipps Plaza and Lenox Square, where he would hand me a set of keys. I would look at him in surprise as he exited the vehicle while the immaculately dressed doorman with a limousine driver hat opened my door. After receiving a generous tip, the doorman would smile knowingly at me and, with a wink, welcome me to my new home, residence of the illustrious Dustin Antonio himself. Well, he probably could do it, too, as he was a super producer to stars. By 1992, he was certainly worth some millions of dollars.

All this nonsense made me miss Tony, who I loved so much and who loved me in return. If he was here, he would surely beat somebody up and take me to safety. But I could never tell him this was how I was living. He would be enraged. Angry with our parents for allowing me to suffer on my own like this. Or, even worse, angry with me for lowering my standards and living in such a deplorable way. He would never understand why I chose this path to freedom.

Was that what I was doing, though? No, of course not. Who was I kidding? I wasn't living a life of real freedom, just another type of bondage. But where could I go next? Who would take me in? What lie could I tell that would be believable enough to get me out of here? I had never been so afraid yet so determined in my life to escape this treatment that I had brought on myself.

My precarious lifestyle caused me to reflect on Daddy and how he, too, led a fractured life he seemed to want to escape from. When I was younger, his drug addiction terrified me. He seemed to morph into the perfect Dr. Jekyll and Mr. Hyde characters when he was high. I got high at least on a weekly basis, but I didn't consider myself like Daddy entirely. I usually stuck to weed because I felt like I could control it. There were no hallucinations or tripping experiences. Just a lot of laughter and eventually sleep.

In addition to drugs, I drank almost every day. I often drank to fall asleep or to make myself relax or, well, for every reason imaginable. Drinking made me feel older—it was how I thought adults were adults. I recall one time I was told that I couldn't handle my liquor, so I drank more and tried really hard to not fall down or do something stupid that would embarrass me later. Turns out I had such a high tolerance that I figured it had to be genetic. There were heavy drinkers on both sides of my family, but Mommy drew the line at herself. She once told me that she didn't want to be a drinker because of what she saw her mother and stepfather go through. I guess I listened to her to an extent because I was determined not to try anything else besides alcohol and weed.

Alcohol. Drugs. Violence, emotional and physical. Infidelity. My family—my parents—had lived a hard marriage. Mommy and Daddy had been married for twenty-three years and their marriage was the worst one that I'd ever heard of or seen. I knew they had separated after I had him locked up and I moved to Atlanta. I was proud of that. Mommy had gotten restraining orders and had the locks changed and everything. But, by herself, she couldn't afford the townhouse's rent, so she was evicted from the place we'd landed at due to Daddy's lack of responsibility to the family.

Ironically, we had found that townhouse through a lady whose husband I'd met at a club one night, when me and Carla were hanging out. He didn't wear a ring, so I got his number and began seeing him. One evening, he took me to dinner but claimed he needed to get something he left at his house. When we got there, he invited me in. It was a set-up; I had fallen for his ruse, but I didn't know how to back out of this obvious trap. Although I liked him a lot, he seemed way too focused on rushing us into his room. All I could think was, *What happened to dinner?*

Then we heard someone enter the house and a woman's voice yelled, "Horace!" I freaked out, grabbing my things hastily. "Who is that?" I cried.

"She has a gun," he answered, tense, as he pulled me along. "Let's go out the back door."

Once outside, I didn't know what to think. I was stunned, upset, scared—and very angry at the idiot for not wearing his ring or bothering to tell me he was a married man. I was infuriated that he made the story up about needing to get something from his home, and I was mad at myself for not staying in the car and demanding to go to dinner like we planned. We argued all the way back to my parents' apartment.

I called his house as soon as I got in, aware it would be a while before he got back to his place. I was nervous, scared stiff, but I felt that poor woman needed to know everything that had happened.

As I dialed his number, I felt physically ill. "Hello?" a woman answered with caution.

"Um, hi. You…you don't know me, but I just left your house."
I could hear her gasp and cover her mouth. "Uh-huh." was all she said.

"I'm really sorry, ma'am, but I'm fifteen and I didn't know your husband was married.

He lied to me and told me we were going to dinner."

"Your parents would let you go out with a grown man?"

I spoke quickly, the words tumbling out, "Well, my dad isn't home a lot, and I didn't tell my mother the truth—but I have to tell you what happened because you deserve to know. Your husband told me we were going to dinner. I met him several months ago at RJ's by the Lake. When he picked me up tonight, he told me we needed to stop by his house because he needed to pick something up and—"
She interrupted me, "I can't believe him."

I hurried to finish, "So, I agreed, but it felt weird. He was rushing me and pulled me into his, well, your bedroom and that's when you came home and he said you had a gun. Ma'am, I'm really, really sorry!" I began to cry uncontrollably.

"Sweetheart," she calmly replied, "you had no business in a grown man's home, but I'm sorry this happened to you. I'm really sorry."

She told me she would deal with him and asked if I wanted to help. I gave her my number so we could stay in touch. She then revealed she wanted to set him up for this stunt. Full of hate for this two-timer, I said I'd help her any way I could.

I told Mommy what happened, who was shocked at the news, but she also agreed to help this woman, whose name was Misty.

She came by on Saturday and said Horace had been shaking in his boots all week. She'd received flowers and chocolates at her job. But this wasn't his first rodeo. Horace had cheated on her before with a college student from their alma mater. She said he denied it, but she didn't have hard evidence like she did with me calling her.

They were college sweethearts who graduated from Texas A&M. He had landed a good job at Electronic Data Systems in Plano, and she worked as an engineer for another big company. They'd been married for six years and had a four-year-old, but that hadn't stopped him from being unfaithful.

At our apartment, the Misty, Mommy, and I sat around the table while Misty dialed her home phone number. We all stared at the speaker as the phone rang. I was scared to death that we were actually doing this, but I wanted him to pay for what he did—we all did.

"Good morning, the Bronner residence," said the man on the other end. It was definitely Horace.

I felt my stomach tighten and suddenly felt like I needed to rush to the bathroom. I ignored my biology and listened in, my lips pressed tightly in effort to keep silent.

"Yeah, hi, babe, it's me." Misty started off nonchalant and then laid out the facts. "You know how I have been silent this week. I haven't really been able to say much. Well, it has taken me everything to hold it together. You know how when you got home last Friday night, I was calm, even though you lied to me about what happened. You told me you had to go to the hospital, and you pretended not to hear me calling for you."

"Yeah, baby," he replied, trying to sound casual, "I wasn't feeling well. Remember, I even followed up with my doctor this week."

"Horace, it reminded me of last year when you and that girl from our college were writing each other love letters. You behaved the same exact way with the expensive dinner and sending the flowers to my job and all of that. Remember that, Horace?"

"Baby, what are you getting at?" His voice was nervous but cautious.

"Well, Horace, you wouldn't believe what happened after your ER visit. A young lady called me and told me all about your real sickness. What are the chances of that, baby?" She raised her voice and scolded him, "And don't even think of lying to me, Horace, because I'm sitting here with her mother and we are going to hang you. You will lose everything for this, you unfaithful idiot!"

Encouraged, I chimed in, "You should be ashamed of yourself!"

He ignored what I said, but I could hear his voice beginning to quiver.

"Baby—" Misty quickly cut him off, "Don't call me 'baby'."

He was silent for a moment. "Misty, what can I do?"

"You can pack your bags and find another place to call home—and forget about the townhouse because I already changed the locks and filed for a restraining order. If you so much as set foot on that property, you will go to jail. I *dare* you to try me. I am divorcing you because you are not satisfied with what I have to give. *It's over*, buddy." And with that, she hung up the phone.

Misty looked at Mommy for a moment and then broke out sobbing. In response, Mommy hugged her like a daughter, rocking her back and forth.

Misty looked to Mommy for support during the entire divorce proceedings. Mommy, in turn, assured her that she wouldn't press charges for Horace's actions with me because the couple had a son and it wouldn't be right to have the father locked up when he could help provide for the family.

It eventually became common for Misty to come over from time to time. Often, she had little Horace Jr. with her, who looked just like his father. Sometimes, she brought groceries for us. Our finances were terrible due to Daddy blowing the money on drugs and other women, so Misty's aid was a godsend.

Mommy and Misty struck up a sincere friendship through all of this. A kindred spirit, Mommy understood what it was like to be a woman scorned; she had caught Daddy cheating on many occasions. I learned the details of these encounters when Mommy shared her marriage war stories during Misty's visits.

One day, Mommy confided to Misty that we had an eviction notice and Mommy didn't know what we were going to do. Then, a few days later, Misty surprised us with bags and bags of groceries.
Stunned, I just couldn't believe it. I went out to grab the remaining bags

from Misty's car. When I came back in, Mommy and Misty were crying and hugging.

Misty explained in between sniffles, "The judge granted me the house and the townhouse.

He's keeping our vacation property and his car and a few other things that I don't care about. You should have seen the look on his face."
I hadn't realized they had so much property.

She then handed Mommy a set of keys, and Mommy began to cry, "Misty, what is this for?"

"It's for helping me through this. Your husband is just like him, you know. You need to leave him for good, Ann."

As they embraced, I couldn't believe what I was hearing. We were going to have a place to stay after all…!

After receiving a hug from her, I thanked Misty for the food and began putting it all in the refrigerator. While they said their goodbyes, I hoped Mommy would take her advice and truly leave Daddy. This was a golden opportunity, but I wasn't sure if she would take advantage of it.

A while later, Mommy came into the kitchen, still wiping her tears away. "God works in mysterious ways, Keeya. Don't worry about Daddy. I've learned what to say and what to keep quiet from him."
I was relieved and wondered how she always seemed to know what I was thinking.

On the Run

My mind switched back to the present. I hadn't spoken to Mommy in several weeks. I wasn't eager to do it now, but I longed to hear her voice. I needed something familiar. She was my mother and I was her baby, even though we didn't understand each other all of the time. She loved me and I knew it. I took a deep breath and dialed zero for the operator.

"Southwestern Bell operator," came the polite voice on the other end, "how can I connect your call?"

"Yes, I'd like to make a collect call from this number." I swallowed the lump in my throat. "My name is Keeya."

"Just a moment. Thank you for contacting Southwestern Bell... Your call is connected." The phone rang twice, and she picked up to answer. "Hello?"

"This is the Southwestern Bell operator. I have a collect call from Keeya. Do you accept the charges?"

"Well, yes, I do." A moment later, "Hi, sweetie, how are you doing?"

I instantly smiled at the sound of her kind, loving voice. "Hey, Mommy!" I managed. "I'm great, how are you?"

"Well, not too good," she confessed. "I left your father shortly after you left. I had filed for a restraining order, but knowing him, I didn't feel safe living there. You remember Don from *Dallas Weekly*? You know, the editor?"

"Yes, Mommy, of course I remember him. I knew him first."

"Well, he and his wife invited me to come live with them. I told them I didn't know where you were, and I told them what happened with your father."

I sighed but let her keep talking.

"Where are you, by the way? Do you still work for that studio company with that millionaire? Your boss is so nice that he would send you home to be with me for Christmas. God bless his soul!"

I had forgotten which lie I had told her, so I went with the one she'd remembered. "Oh, yeah, he's great."

"I always knew you would be fine. I put some fight in you, didn't I?"

"Yeah, I'm fighting every day, Mommy. Don't worry about me. So, how long do you plan to stay there?"

"Oh, I don't know. I'm bartering my time here. I'm making some draperies out of some old sheets for a client and showing his wife how to rearrange things to make what they have lovely."

"I'm not shocked at all," I laughed. No matter where Mommy was, she would find a way to beautify her surroundings. She hadn't changed a bit. I switched the subject to something I'd seriously been

pondering. "So, Mommy, I need to know something."
"Yes, baby, what is it?"

I breathed in, then asked, "Would you consider moving here? We could share a one-bedroom apartment and start our lives over. I really *cannot* stand my roommates." I stopped myself—I'd nearly made the lie even bigger just then!
"Oh, you met some young ladies there?" she asked in a pleased, sing-song voice. "Yeah," I promptly replied, "but they go to the Art Institute of Atlanta and they're pretty wild. Too many strange men in the apartment." I bit back a nervous laugh. "I don't feel safe sometimes."
"You mean you would want me to move in with you? I thought you hated me."

"No, Mommy, I love you. I just hate Daddy, and I never want you to go back to him. If you do, he might kill you! He tried to kill me that one time and-and if you weren't there to take those hits for me, I probably would have died!"

I realized I had raised my voice. After regaining control of myself, I asked more calmly, "Mommy, how *are* you doing from all of that, anyway?"

"Keeya, I thought my neck was broken, but the doctor said it was just severely sprained. I've had some of the worst headaches since that fight, but I'd do it again if I had to." I could hear the conviction in her voice. "He was going to have to kill me first before I'd *ever* let him come to you."

Tears streamed down my face at her words. I sniffled and could hear her doing the same. "Keeya," she finally said, "I'll only come if you want me to. I'll do anything I can to make sure you're safe. I don't like hearing that you feel unsafe. I raised a good girl. Those hussies need to learn a thing or two from you. By the way, have you met any more celebrities at those events you go to?"

"Well, it wasn't at an event, but I was at the nail shop and met Chilli from TLC. She knows my boss because he helped produce some songs on their album."

"Did you tell her you work for him?" "Uh, no, I didn't."

"Well, why not?"

"Mommy, it's not important. It just slipped my mind. But here's what happened." And I proceeded to tell Mommy all about it.

Like I said, I did have the pleasure of meeting Chilli of TLC. It was not through Dustin or any of his entourage but across town at Hollywood Nails of all places. I had just picked out a beautiful sheer coral color for my long overdue manicure. Because there was a wait, I checked out the nearby candy machine that was stocked with M&Ms. As I turned the knob for my treat of colorful joy, I heard someone come near. I looked up and I immediately recognized her—Chilli from TLC! She looked at me casually when our eyes met and she smiled. I had learned from all of the events I had attended that celebrities wanted to be treated like real people. I found that they would be near you a little longer if you didn't act so starstruck.

"Are those M&Ms?" she asked inquisitively.

"Yeah, they're my favorite." I was nervous but excited at the same time. *C'mon, play it cool, Keeya.*

"Can I have one?" She wrinkled her nose up like a little kid. "Sure!" I exclaimed with excitement.

She reached into my palm, grabbed an M&M, smiled her thanks, and ate it.

I couldn't believe it. Chilli of TLC was a regular, nice person—who just happened to be one third of my favorite girl group ever! Then she turned around and sat down to get her manicure, telling the nail tech not to cut her cuticles but to push them back.

Mommy seemed pleased with my story. It was the first time I'd told her something true in a long time. Not that I could ever tell her the truth behind meeting Dustin or living with the groups he was producing. I had told her that I had a part-time job as a hip-hop dancer or something. Despite this, I was genuinely happy that she was deciding to move here. Finally, I could live something of a normal life again.

The chance meeting with Chilli had left me hopeful. I wanted to be somebody. I just didn't know how to pull myself up by my bootstraps and make something of myself. I started getting manicures and asking the nail tech to push *my* cuticles back—that was a start!

I knew I needed help in the self-esteem department. For a split second, I thought about trying to reconnect with Chilli to ask for help. I blew that idea off, though, because I would have to tell the truth and risk looking like the average groupie—not the most wholesome rep to have.

But with Mommy moving to Atlanta, I wouldn't need any more help. We had made it through worse situations. We would be free to live on our own, away from Daddy and everything I'd been facing. We would be just fine.

I had finally reached the point of being beyond fed up with my current living arrangement. There was no way but down if I lived around the boys. Even though nobody would possibly believe me, I really did not like my life. The moments of 'fun' were deeply overshadowed by the promiscuous price I paid to have them. I wasn't enjoying the feeling of self-loathing. My alcohol and drug addictions were my only escape, but even that satisfaction was short-lived. While it was nice to see the clout that some people had, it was a miserable reality that I had none of my own. I would never be a real singer or professional dancer, so why was I still here?

I eventually became best friends with a young woman named Nikki. She was friends with the crew and a fellow participant at Diamonds and Pearls. She was roommates with another lady named Cindy and they attended the Art Institute of Atlanta for fashion design (they were the ones I led Mommy to believe I lived with). I knew they were quickly becoming people that I could trust.

As it turns out, Nikki pieced together what was going on before I chose to say anything; every time she came around to visit, she seemed to want to protect me. Because I felt she could see right through my lies, I told her the truth about my age before anyone else. I later told Cindy, and they were both very worried for me like sisters would be.

Even though she was struggling financially, too, Nikki was

passionately against my living situation and she always schooled me on how I should be treated. While she didn't know the depth of my experiences, that didn't stop her from voicing her mind.

"Keeya, I know they have sisters and mothers. What idiots. I don't know how, but you need to get outta there, like, fast!"

"Yeah, I know," I mumbled, aware her words were true.

"I need to tell Dustin you need a place to live," she continued. "He has enough money to put you up somewhere."

Encouraged by my friends' support, I wanted to live with them in their dorm, but they would risk being put out. They also had a roommate who was not very friendly, so that was off the table.

While I hadn't been able to figure out where to go next, I knew that I had reached the end of my rope. I had frequent crying spells and I was arguing with everybody almost every day. As the days and weeks flew by, I grew restless waiting for Mommy to get her affairs in order. I decided that she was taking too long, so I chose to tell the groups the truth about my age. Maybe I shouldn't have been surprised, but no one was particularly astonished by the reveal, and one guy even admitted he'd already known how old I was. With my secret officially out, though, I knew that I had to leave. Relieved to be out of this situation, I was fine with whatever my exit would bring. It appeared as though things couldn't get any worse, especially with this apathetic crowd.

Although Nikki and Cindy weren't viable options, they weren't the only choice I had available to me at the time. In addition to these girls, there was another young woman named

Rae Rae. Compared to the others, she was a totally different story. Like me, she moved from pillar to post. She seemed to live any place where she could lay her head long enough, going wherever the wind blew her. Nikki and Cindy thought she was constantly on the run, as if there was something she was trying to escape. She also was certainly the type who knew how to play the promiscuity 'game' to her advantage. She happened to have a young son, but God only knows who was taking care of him.

Aware of my thinking, my friends both warned me not to even think of living with Rae Rae, but I didn't listen. Although I was grateful for their concern, I didn't feel they *really* understood what I was going through. But Rae Rae, the closest thing I had to a kindred spirit in my situation, probably did. Maybe she thought we were alike, too. She claimed to have a brother who would let us both live with him. My desperation won over my skepticism of the offer and I went to live with her.

What a disaster. Rae Rae had to be the most unstable woman on the planet, next to me of course. She was constantly in transition, from checking into a hotel to getting put up in an apartment every few months. She also kept introducing me to new 'customers', even though she knew I was wanting to put that life behind me. And it seems that while I had hoped to receive empathy from her, she couldn't care less. She merely saw me as a source of funds, stealing money from me when I was just as financially desperate. In short, rooming with her had become a bad idea. There was no firm security in what was revealed to be a very unpredictable life.

Despite the Rae Rae drama, with Mommy still planning to come and my age out in the open, I still needed money to be able to move and get out on my own. Saturday night, fortunately, was on the way. It was my favorite night of the week because of the miniskirt contest. The prize for first place was $500. I had Nikki pick me up in her cute, black Nissan Sentra. From her creole complexion to her curly waves that were always perfectly sewn in, I could tell Nikki had it going on tonight!

In no time, we pulled up to Diamonds and Pearls. In the neon light, in addition to her great hair, I could see Nikki had on her black latex Daisy Dukes, which she paired with a black leather motorcycle jacket. After she freshened up her signature red matte lipstick, we headed to the club.

As we walked, I adjusted my black dress that kept rising in the back. It was purposefully a size too small, with a v plunge down my back. My heels were three inches high so that I could dance with ease. I wore my hair straight and jet-black, complete with a hairpiece that made me look a lot older.

I had to win tonight. I needed money for my next move. And when Mommy came, things would definitely be better.

Jetson, the assistant manager, held the door open for us. He was handsome, with skin the color of a Hershey chocolate bar and coal-black curly hair. He seemed like a gangster who ran numbers in the '40s. Very clean-cut and old-school savvy, but the look on his face had 'player' written all over it.

"Hello, ladies," he said warmly. "Keeya, you gettin' that money tonight? You know you gonna win!" He laughed as we walked in.

"I'm gonna try, Jetson," I answered, smiling.

Nikki followed me to the steps of the VIP area, where I flashed my card, and we headed up the steps. As usual, we looked around to see who was there. Not many people were up there yet. It was only a little after ten o'clock.

"So, Keeya, you're entering the contest tonight, right?" asked Nikki as she motioned for the bartender to come to our end of the bar. The man held up his finger to signal that he would be there in a moment.

I leaned on the counter. "Chris, don't keep us waiting!" I called playfully, but he knew I was just messing with him. It was my way of saying hi.

"I would never do that to pretty ladies like you," he answered, but he continued his conversation and made drinks for nearby patrons.

Antsy from waiting, I stretched my legs, pumping myself up for tonight. "Okay, girl, I need to sign up for the contest."

"Okay, sweetie," Nikki replied as she drummed her fingers on the counter. I won the contest that night.

Chapter 10

The Masquerade

I don't know if leaving the boys was ultimately a smart move or not. All I know is that I realized I *was* able to control my environment, which was priceless to me. I quickly learned to block the memories I'd made with the guys out of my head whenever I was reminded of those times of debauchery and mayhem. But the entertainment lifestyle was a residue not easily cleansed. In a warped way, it had become an avenue toward obtaining security, my chips in a high-stakes game of survival. Youth and beauty seemed to pay dividends that would get me to my goals much quicker than any other way. Because my outlook had been marred, I didn't know how to view life through any other lens.

I was fortunate, though, to have gotten to know other people who I felt I could explain my true story to. One such person was Big Will, the manager of Diamonds and Pearls. He had so many connections to entertainers, drug dealers, lawyers, and all sorts of people who partied there. He took a liking to me when I kept winning the miniskirt contests he put on. I was good for business. Everyone liked him because he was the kind of person who paid attention to you the moment you were in front of him, making you feel that you were very important to him. I could have anything I wanted from Big Will. Knowing that, I often took full advantage and we became closer than we should have.

As a result, our relationship became short-lived once I became pregnant.

"I know you aren't trying to have this baby?" He had asked it like a question, but there was a controlling undercurrent to his words. "You know I have four kids, and I'm being investigated because of this crazy lawyer I've done business with."

"Crazy lawyer?" I asked.

"Yeah, Keeya, I might be locked up. The club is in big trouble, too. I'm not going to be a good father to the kids I have, much less another one. I might be locked up for a very long time, Keeya—a very long time. This is all a bunch of crap that this dude got me into. He's the crazy lawyer I'm talking about. It's all over the news and now I'm taking heat."

My heart sank into my stomach.

This lawyer was under investigation for his own wife's murder, which happened last year. I didn't want to think about how someone I was connected to could be involved in such a tragic event. I felt like I didn't want to know any more.

As the full implication of his words sank in, I stared at Big Will and felt hopelessness overcome me. There was no point trying to convince myself that there was anything to our relationship other than a good time gone bad.

And the life that was inside of me was a difficult pill to swallow. This conversation was leading to the beginning and ending of another life. This life would never see the break of day nor would it ever have a say in the discussion of its demise. Within weeks, barely formed, an entire human being would be laid down. Another mistake? Yet another pregnancy? How could I have done this again?

I was convinced that these children would haunt my existence. They already did.

I thought back to Caleb and how my pregnancy made him tell me that my having his child would ruin his life. I had loved him so dearly, I had never wanted to cause him any pain, so I gave in to his request for an abortion. I had sworn to myself that I would never end up in that situation again. However, within a year's time, I was right back where I started. Contemplating the death of one more child conceived carelessly by me and Big Will.

With such a feeling of guilt creeping over me, I was convinced that I was never going to be a mother. Disheartened, I began to sob deeply.

I heard Big Will's Sky pager go off. He checked it, then made a phone call.

I just kept crying, wishing he would reach over and hold me, give me comfort. But he didn't. Inside, I felt cheap, worthless, unimportant. But what should I have expected? This was by no means a relationship based on love. This was all lust and no depth, a cheap thrill. I was so disgusted with myself for living this way.

"We need to go—I have an appointment," Big Will said briskly. He didn't so much as acknowledge my feelings. His casual words left me devastated.

"Jetson will be in touch with you," he continued, "as I know where you can get a procedure done. He'll take you there sometime this week. I'll take care of any expenses."

Something in his voice told me this happened often with Big Will. I felt like a client or something. Take care of any expenses? This wasn't a mere business transaction. This was a human life inside me.

His coldness confirmed more than I wanted to admit to myself. All the free drinks in the world would not be enough to extinguish the guilt that had become my garment of choice. I had become a bad person.

How could I have been so careless with my life?

After the procedure, things felt awkward when I was at the club, though Big Will always coolly acknowledged me with a drink from the bartender. They all seemed to know the look on my face was one of many they'd seen before. Sometimes, Jetson, who had picked me up from the clinic, would lean over and whisper for me to get over him. Everyone had to know about my failed affair with Big Will by now. Embarrassed, I stopped entering the miniskirt contests altogether.

Despite our severed relationship, Big Will introduced me to a woman he thought would be able to help me in the long term. Summer Breeze, though short like me, was bowlegged and about thirty pounds heavier. Her thin hair was always in a ponytail swooped over to one side. I frequently saw her in nice leather jackets with skintight jeans and about ten gold necklaces in varied lengths. Her earrings were like the pretty gold ones that Mommy and I would covet as we browsed the Service Merchandise catalogs, and her three rings, one a ruby atop a yellow gold band and two diamond-clustered, gleamed expensively.

Though she never wore any makeup, she owned a beauty salon on paper, which was a cover-up business for what she really did.

Breeze also drove a funny-looking car. Maybe it was a Dodge or something. It looked like what a retired couple might drive. It was tan and very clean, both inside and out. This transportation was yet another arrangement Big Will made for me. I guess, in his own odd way, he was concerned for my well-being.

Over time, I found Breeze was very observant and calculating, like there was a paranoia about her that seemed unnatural, eerie, even cold-blooded. Before I officially met her, I actually had seen her at the club on occasion and she was always alone. Sometimes, Big Will would send her a drink or they would chat. Whatever they did seemed to be important.

When we finally met face-to-face, me with my green travel bag and few personal effects, she with her devil-may-care ease, it was after hours. Something about our meeting felt weird, but I couldn't pinpoint it. It was like I was being tested and groomed for yet another masquerade.

"Hi, there. Keeya, right?" She looked me over like I was on sale, giving me a once-over before commanding suddenly, "Turn around."

"Turn around?" I asked with my eyebrows raised.

"That's what I said, isn't it?" She enunciated 'it' with an attitude, as if to say I had better do what she asked or else.

As I awkwardly rotated, she took a long drag from the cigarette she'd just lit. "So, what has Big Will told you about me?"

"He just said you could help me," I answered uneasily.

She blew the smoke to one side and looked intently at me as if making a decision. "Mm-hmm. Get in the car and I'll tell you all about me—and a few things about you, too." She cackled drily as if she had just said something funny. I guess it was funny to her.

Obediently, I threw my bag in the back seat and put my other belongings in the trunk before getting in alongside her.

"Put on your seat belt, Keeya. I don't need the cops pulling me over." I complied and we drove in silence for a bit, heading for her place.

"You're not the age you said you were, Keeya," she said, coming straight to the point. "You're a hustler like me, and I like that about you."

I formed my lips to correct her with a lie, but she stopped me with a keen side glance. "Baby, I can help you, but you have to be honest with me and willing to do what I tell you to do. That is if you want to make money and take care of yourself." Feeling put on the spot, I took a deep breath and watched her drive.

"How old are you, really?" Although she kept her eyes on the road, her expression was dead serious.

I felt like I didn't want to—couldn't—lie to her. She would detect it. "Sixteen," I finally admitted, "about to turn seventeen in March."

"Pieces," she named me with a sly grin, "yeah, I gotta watch you." She began to laugh again and took a long drag from her cigarette. As I watched her smoke languidly, a loathsome feeling came over me.

Two days after having gotten situated, it was in the early

morning hours when I walked into her room, which was so dimly lit that I had to walk slowly so that I didn't bump into anything. Breeze was sitting in the middle of her king-size canopy bed, bent over low with a big hardcover book propped up by her knees. Completely oblivious to my presence, she made a loud sniffing noise, turning her head to the side and letting out an extended loud moan. Worried that she was sick or something, I quietly made it to the edge of her bed. As I moved, I saw the single candle by her bedside flicker as if it noticed someone new was in the room.

She tilted her head back and took another deep sniff, and, still unaware of my presence, began to laugh. I quickly glanced at the book as it slid off one of her knees: being used as a table, the book supported a small mirror, which was covered with a powdery substance that was divided into even white rows. As the book slid off its perch, the powder scattered across the reflective surface like grainy stars.

I wiped the sleep from my eyes, sickening with realization. I knew exactly what she was doing, but I didn't know how to confront her. Before I could think or do anything, her eyes caught my slight movement and she looked up, startled.

Words failed to form in my mouth as Breeze set the book and the cocaine-dressed mirror aside. She raised herself up and began to straighten her clothing.

"You haven't been here two days and you're already snoopin' around and spyin' on me, huh?" She cocked her head curiously in my direction, her look causing me to stiffen. "What's next, you gon' try and judge me in my own house where I pay the bills?"

"I-I-I couldn't sleep, so I saw that you were up, and-and..." Words still escaped me. I couldn't figure out what I was supposed to say. It was after 4 a.m. and I just wanted to sleep.

"So, were you going to say something, Pieces?" A smile slowly slid across her face. "I feel too good at the moment to be mad at you. Besides, you're going to make me plenty of money!" She gave a dry chuckle and patted the bed. "Have a seat."

"What do you mean? How am I going to do that?" I began to feel my blood pressure rise.

So far, this woman hadn't told me anything about what was expected of me. And I had a sneaking suspicion I probably wasn't going to like it.

"Oh, Big Will didn't tell you about my lingerie modeling business? I have several and I'll take you around to them tomorrow. They'll like you—new, young. Huh, I guess that's all it takes to make money in this business." She shrugged lightly, lit a cigarette, and kept looking at me from the corners of her eyes.

Suddenly aware I might need more info, Breeze reached over and gave me a newspaper that had what appeared to be a classified ad circled in red:

Are you wanting to find new ways to relax?
If so, please meet our young and professional models from all over the world!
They won't disappoint!

In shock from the words I was reading, I tried to wrap my mind around what it would mean to work at a place that modeled lingerie. Was this even legal?

"Snap out of it, honey," Breeze said, catching my dazed look as she resumed her previous position. "Ain't nothin' free. You wanna live here? Then you have to help me keep food on the table. Big Will told me you have skills on the dance floor. This will be easier than that. Less competition. I make sure not to have the same ethnicity working at the same location and time slot."

"Okay, so where do I get the clothes?" I asked halfheartedly.

"I supply the lingerie and costumes, you just wear them for the clients," she answered matter-of-factly, squinting at me as she took a long drag on her cigarette. "Now, if you'll excuse me…"

She looked down at her lap, where one scattered line had been re-formed next to another.

She bent over the mirror and took a long sniff, leaning her head back into the pillows that supported her.

Chapter 11

Absconded

When she arrived home one day, Breeze looked like she needed sleep. I could tell her drug addiction was getting worse. She'd begun to forget, for example, about the doctor's appointments for her aging aunt, who suffered mental health issues.

"You look beat," I commented. I wanted to say that the dark circles under her eyes made her look frightening, but I knew better.

She walked in, looking behind her as if someone might be close behind. She went straight to the living room window, peeking out quickly before she came over to me.

"Have you noticed any cars with men in them, just sitting outside for hours at a time?" she asked me, narrowing her eyes as if to detect if I was telling the truth or not.

"No, I haven't," I said, honestly.

"If you do anything stupid to take me away from Auntie and Anton, there is no clue what might happen to you!"

Inwardly, I shook my head at this sudden outburst. Such off-the-wall threats were the norm for Breeze, though I doubted I'd ever get used to them. It was only a matter of time before she would lose her mind completely or that something bad would happen here.

She walked over to the cordless phone and lifted it off the base.

She began scrolling through the numbers, stopping at one that got her attention.

"When did this guy call?" she asked, looking up at me. "Around twelve."

"I see there's a call from one of the numbers I told you not to answer around that time.

Remember me telling you about the police station prefixes?"

I gulped and looked down lamely at the floor, hating myself. How could I have been so dumb?

"How many times do I need to tell you not to answer certain phone calls?" Her voice was at a fever pitch, confirmation that I'd blown it.

"For the last time, Keeya, if you aren't sure, don't answer the phone! Now we're going to need to not answer the door when this idiot shows up, so we don't risk anything today. This means I'll have to move our location, and I can't make money if we have to move all of the time!"

Feeling guilty enough already, I tuned her tirade out. I couldn't believe I made such a stupid mistake. I went over to the sofa and sat down.

"Do you understand me, Pieces?"

I nodded and looked away, preparing to sulk. Then the doorbell rang.

Wide-eyed, I glanced at Breeze for instructions. She put her finger to her lips and mouthed, *Be quiet.*

The doorbell rang again, and she slowly looked out of the peephole. I stood stock-still, my heart pounding in my ears.

She stood there in silence for a few minutes, then she rushed over to the living room window, which faced the parking lot. "Mm-hmm," she confirmed, turning back to me once the threat was gone. "I can smell a cop a mile away. Lesson number two, Pieces, don't answer the phone if the caller's number is private, not listed, or if the prefix is 612 or 613. Period."

I nodded, letting out a breath I realized I'd been holding with a whoosh. A potential crisis had just been averted.

As time passed, I realized that, although she was almost like a mother hen to me, Breeze had no patience with anyone except her Aunt Agnes. When Aunt Agnes would run out of her medication, for example, all hell would break loose at home. The last time that woman ran out of her meds, Breeze and I drove up to find her butt-naked hanging Christmas lights in the rain.

When Breeze asked her what was going on, the elderly woman just cracked up laughing and kept climbing the ladder.

Despite the occasional difficulty, Breeze took care of Agnes as she was able. In the morning, she would prepare the daily meals for her aunt and make sure she took her medication. For the most part, Aunt Agnes could be left alone for hours at a time. Often, the medication made her sleepy, so she would curl up on the sofa and doze while her daily soap operas played on TV. The business took in its last client at 6 p.m., so we were home around 7:30 p.m. every night. That was just in time for Aunt Agnes to eat dinner and take her last dose of medication before her bedtime.

And while Breeze appeared to have a soft spot for Agnes, she didn't outwardly extend that consideration to her own son, Anton, who was rarely graced with a smile. An only child, he had seen too much in his fifteen years. I felt bad for him because he had to maintain the wholesome lie that his mother ran an innocent beauty salon. Despite the shadiness he indirectly propagated, Anton seemed to be an otherwise good kid. He played football and even made the honor roll every now and then. When he wasn't playing video games on his Sega, he talked on the phone to his girlfriend. Since he wasn't home most of the time, there didn't appear to be much interaction between family members.

I felt like I observed this family almost like a wildlife biologist studying a family of near-extinct bears. I never felt like I was a part of their lives but rather like I was only close enough to see how this family lived from day to day. I often wondered why Breeze was so trusting of me and so distrusting of others.

As for me, I stayed in the guest room and kept to myself most of the time. I often thought about Big Will. Had he done me a favor by setting me up this way? I guess I couldn't expect more, given my reputation. Oddly enough, living here was the most normal I had felt—in the sense of pulling up to a house every night and having my own room and all. It was just my day job that was abnormal. I just couldn't seem to figure 'normal' out in that department. I wasn't even sure if I was capable of it.

I longed for the day when Mommy would be there with me. Even with all her flaws, I knew she loved me. I never had to guess that.

But, for the time being, Breeze was the closest thing I had to a mother, though a rough one; and as a result, Anton naturally made me think of Tony. They had similar mannerisms.
Neither of them seemed to be moved by much, and they both knew how to keep themselves preoccupied for hours at a time by working on some project or another.

Although I missed Mommy bunches, I missed Tony more. We didn't talk very much anymore. I was more to blame for that. I didn't want to talk to him with my life being a wreck and because of how I was ashamed I was of my choices. But I could've really used the laughter and joy he brought to my life when we were kids. For so many years, I had wanted to be just like him. And now was no different. I mean, what would he think of me now? My longing to be normal (and respected even more so) was intense.

Heck, I remember when we lived in Columbus, where some of my best childhood experiences were. Anything Tony did, I tried to emulate. He loved the Wonder Twins—so did I. Tony signed up for karate classes at St. Stephen's Community Center—so did I. It didn't matter what he took an interest in, I was by his side showing just as much interest. His opinion mattered to me because I knew how much he loved me and would try to protect me from other people, even from Daddy.

Come to think of it, Tony often looked out for me on the playground and won several fights for me. Though, well, one such fight didn't turn out so well. Back in Kindergarten at McGuffey Elementary, I remember when we all used to play on the playgrounds and in the schoolyard. During recess one sunny day, we were all outside, a chaotic mix of students from multiple grades. Although Tony was usually nearby, this time I didn't know where he was.

I was swinging on the swings and fully enjoying myself. I leaned way back, lifting my legs up to gain momentum, and then I leaned forward, bringing my legs back underneath me as I sailed through the air. The wind whipped by my ears and across my face, the sensation exhilarating. Sometimes, I would close my eyes and become dizzy, then I'd jump off and run in zigzag circles until I fell in laughter—only to get back on and do it again and again.

I noticed a few older kids getting close to the swings. I didn't pay them much attention until one of them came over to my swing and yanked the chain, causing me to slip out of the seat and crumple to the ground.

"Hey, I need this swing. You've been on it long enough!" she yelled, while her friends laughed.

Jolted out of my happy daydreaming, pain stinging my shins, I glared up at her. "I'm going to tell my big brother on you and he's going to beat you up!" I spat back.

It didn't matter to me that she was bigger than him. I was going to find him. She was going to get it.

I quickly jumped up, shouldered my backpack, and ran around the yard looking for Tony. I saw a couple of kids walking up ahead but I kept running, yelling, "Tooonnnnyyyy!" I was out of breath, but I yelled out one more time, "Tooonnnnyyy!"

The kids up ahead stopped and, as I got closer, I noticed they were Tony and his friend, Troy.

I ran up and hugged him, trying to catch my breath. Tony asked me immediately, "What's wrong, Keeya?"

Panting with my hands on my knees, I managed to tell him about the big girl who pulled me off the swing. I must have lied and said the girl purposefully hurt me. The next thing I knew, he said, "Show me this girl."

"She's at the school playground," I reported. "Let's go over there."

When we arrived at the playground, I pointed to my aggressor, who was swinging by herself merrily. I remained at a distance in fear and anticipation, watching Tony stride toward her purposefully.

Suddenly, they had gotten into a scuffle. She was so much bigger than I had realized—practically twice his size! From what I could glimpse, Tony had managed to get a few good hits in—then in one move, she picked him up and slammed him into the sticker bushes.

Shocked, I took off running all the way home. Tony followed about ten minutes later, the look of defeat in his eyes.

I looked at him, teary-eyed. "I'm sorry, Tony."

He glanced at me, scratched up from the bushes, and said with a half-smile, "It's okay, Keeya. Let's go inside."

I kept rehearsing in my mind the good times I'd had with Tony when he had still lived at home. Even with all the foolishness we had to endure, we always found a way to laugh. Ever since I had arrived at Atlanta, whenever I felt depressed, I would summon these thoughts and memories to cheer myself up. Thoughts of Tony usually comforted me, but now, after moving from Big Will to Breeze and her 'business', those same thoughts now burdened me.

Over the next few months, Breeze's health continued to decline. The drugs were taking their toll on her. She began giving me more responsibility: at the shop, the girls now turned their money in to me, for example, and I no longer had to 'work' like they did. I guess I considered it a kind of promotion. I just collected money all day, watched TV, and turned the cash over to Breeze at the end. Sometimes, she would forget to pick me up from the shop. Secretly, I was okay with her forgetfulness because I didn't have to deal with her paranoia of the cops.

I could hardly wait to see Mommy. There was such a sense of relief just knowing that she would be in town. I felt like I was being rescued, only I couldn't tell her why. I'm sure she understood the obvious—that I was too young to be alone out here. And such a move was good for her, too. She had had so many years of abuse and mental drain that she was as fragile as an egg. I pieced together that her deepest concern was whether Tony and I saw her as a success or failure in life. If I even hinted at the latter, her face would drop into an expression of defeat. To see her like that made me feel an ache in my heart so deep that I felt like my chest would cave under the weight of the emotion.

In a major way, I had left home for both my peace of mind and hers. I had known deep down that if I left home, eventually she would follow. With Tony married and on his own and with me out of the house, she wouldn't have a reason to stay. I felt proud that at least that much of my plan worked.

I remember the day when her bus finally, *finally* rolled into Atlanta.

I gotta admit the event made me think back to when I had done the same thing. It had been almost a year since I had walked into this city so bright-eyed and optimistic. I had had no idea what my life would become. I'd just showed up to see if I could find something like normal.

I don't know why I felt normal was possible because nothing in my life ever seemed to come close to fitting that description. Even now, with Mommy arriving in town, my life wasn't normal. Far from it! But, despite my reality, my hope was rekindled with just the fact of her finally being here. Maybe we could find normal together?

The doors opened and people filed off the bus. In no time, I saw Mommy step down and I rushed over to hug her, oblivious to the strangers around us. We rocked back and forth, blocking some passengers from moving by us, but we didn't stop our embrace until we were satisfied.

"I really missed you, Mommy!" I exclaimed with genuine excitement.

"I missed you, too, sweetie!" Her eyes danced as she scanned my face, and my smile assured her that I was okay.

"I got rid of everything, Keeya," she continued, somewhat giddy. "I just have these two bags. I'm ready for a new start!" She looked weak, tired from the ride, but hopeful. There certainly *was* a spark of hope in her eyes. I hadn't seen her look this way in a long time.

Mommy had arranged through a friend to stay with a lady until she could find a place to live. I always admired how Mommy didn't waste time when she moved to a new city. Within her first week, she had lined up a job as a seamstress at a drapery workroom. The pay was decent, so she would be able to afford an apartment.

In contrast, I had been living any place I could sleep for a few days at a time.

Emboldened by Mommy coming, I had chosen to leave Breeze's house and her employment. I was tired of constantly living with the threat of getting caught up in a prostitution sting and facing jail time. Sleeping on someone's sofa sure beat the dangerous scenarios I was facing by fooling around with Summer Breeze. I joyfully absconded from the trouble that was sure to catch up with me if I continued living there. I waited until she was away before I packed my things and left as quickly as I had arrived—like a strong summer breeze!

Finally, the day came when Mommy and I moved into our own apartment. Our apartment had one bedroom, and the only things we had were our clothes and a few bags of belongings. We were even within walking distance from the North DeKalb Mall, grocery stores, and strip malls, as well as multiple eateries and fast-food restaurants. We slept on the floor for months, but I felt secure and happy at last. Still, I often cried myself to sleep, tormented by the memories of what I endured to get to this point and conflicted by the belief that I couldn't share the truth with Mommy. I often slept right next to her, hoping that I somehow could regain even just a tiny bit of my innocence.

It didn't work. Instead, I just felt more aware of what I had lost in the process of searching for freedom. We got into arguments often, usually because I reconnected with people from Diamonds and Pearls and went out with Nikki. Mommy seemed to be in shock that I was clubbing. (If only she knew how tame it was compared to everything else!) But I felt beyond obeying her. I was only seventeen, but I felt like I was well into my twenties—an adult. After all I had experienced, I felt that I deserved to live how I wanted to on my own terms. I was very obstinate. Looking back, I wish that I had had more respect for her in those moments. Mommy never pushed for too long, instead shrinking back in defeat and looking the other way.

I finally found regular work at Gap, which was located in Underground Atlanta, a historical site that was also local tourist attraction in the downtown area. The Underground, as we would call it, was a really cool shopping mall under Pryor Street and Upper and Lower Alabama Streets. It was almost like a city!

While living with Mom was rockier than I thought it'd be, she was here with me and I wouldn't trade that for anything. Being with her and having a regular job were the closest things I'd ever had to normal—and I loved it!

Chapter 12

Attempting Normalcy

Like I said, living with Mommy had its challenges, but mostly it was a peaceful time when I experienced normalcy. For the first time in a long while, I could relax in waking up and going to bed. I had a real job where I could clock in and talk to people who only wanted to buy clothing.

The Underground was a fun place to work. It had its own charm as an underground shopping mall that looked like a city, complete with streets and gas lamp posts at various corners and vendors lined up on the sidewalks in front of larger walk-in stores. On a Saturday or during the summer, the streets were filled with people crisscrossing back and forth, shopping and taking pictures with each other. There were always tourist families and individuals I could talk to while they browsed for the latest fashions.

I enjoyed working for Gap because it was one of my favorite stores to shop in, and the discount made it the only place I shopped for clothes. On my breaks and at lunchtime, I would walk around, looking through the windows of the boutiques and novelty shops, occasionally going inside to get a closer look at this or that.

The cart businesses were some of the most interesting, trinket-laden structures, attended by one or two people, which you find in a typical mall setting. One time, I noticed right across from Gap was a cart that sold things for people who were left-handed. There were t-shirts with sayings like, "If the right side of the brain controls the left side of the body, then only people who are left-handed are in their right minds." I looked at the knives that were serrated on the opposite side and at the scissors that had the blades switched to accommodate left-handed individuals. I couldn't figure it all out until I picked up a pencil that read *Lefty's Underground Atlanta*.

As I was going through the interesting items, I heard the young man who worked there comment, "Everything you're picking up is with your right hand."

I swung around and smiled at the gentleman, cleverly retorting, "I'm ambidextrous, so I'm qualified to look around."

"Whoa, I'm just pointing out that I noticed you weren't completely left-handed. I'm sorry, let me start over. My name is Juan. And you are?"

He was being quite charming, and I saw how handsome he was, so I adjusted my tone and replied with a smile, "Hi, Juan. My name is Keeya and I work across the street at the Gap." I looked him over and realized he was a bit on the short side for my liking.

"I know where you work," he said, stroking his mustache shadow with a knowing grin on his face. "I see you almost every day." As a customer walked up to the cart, he motioned for me to wait.

Seeing he was busy, I walked back to my store, but not before waving goodbye to him. I smiled, knowing I'd see him again.

It wasn't long before I began taking my breaks over at the Lefty's cart. Juan was so funny and smart. He went to Georgia State

University and was a pre-med student. He was also a vegetarian and cooked some of the most amazing dishes. Most of his family lived in Puerto Rico, but he came to the US as a child and grew up in Atlanta. We became good friends and did almost everything together. As a result, we quickly became romantically involved—something Mommy did not like, mostly because I would sleep over at his place to avoid the hour-long trip between our living spaces.

Eventually, I met Juan's bosses, a husband-and-wife team who'd opened multiple locations in malls in different cities. They were what I considered 'conscience people' and were very intelligent and friendly. I hit it off with them well and struck up a friendship with the wife, Loretta. It wasn't long before I quit my job at Gap and became their employee.

One of the things that attracted me to working for them was that they supported a business owned by black people. Atlanta was full of black entrepreneurs who I admired so much. Mommy had always encouraged me and Tony to pursue business, so working for them was an honor for me. From time to time, Loretta would take me out for lunch. She basically took me under her wing, where I learned what it meant to work hard and smart.

Eventually, Loretta and her husband opened a store in Baltimore, Maryland, offering me the position of assistant manager. I was so excited that I said yes at once. I thought it seemed like such an adult thing to accept a position from a company that was willing to move you to another state. Plus, it gave me a bit of freedom to have my own space and to get away from Mommy's watchful eye. I really loved her, but inside I held on to a twinge of bitterness that came out from time to time. I wanted to live like an adult without the uncertainty of depending on or being tied to someone else. While Mommy was certainly a safe option for me, and I was relieved in many ways to have her to lean on when needed, I wanted to spread my wings more. There was a woman in me who was growing and wanted to get out and see more of the world.

There was the slight issue of Juan, but I found I wasn't deeply in love. Although we were a couple, we were more like best buds. He helped me to enjoy life, but I didn't want to be held too tightly. We agreed to keep in touch, and as I thanked him for the introduction to Loretta and her husband, we knew it was time for me to move on. Fortunately, he was cordial, so there was no drama for me to deal with.

Telling Mommy was a bit more challenging. I felt, though, she would be fine on her own. She didn't have Daddy to keep her down, and with me gone, she'd have less of a headache. She would be free to live her life on her terms now.

My new life started when we pulled into the familiar Greyhound bus station.

Surprisingly, Mommy was more supportive of me moving than for *my* reasons for moving. She had met Loretta and liked her. She felt confident that I would be under Loretta's supervision while we established the new store. I had done my part, too, having taken time to search for rooms to rent until I found one that was a nice temporary fit. Once I saved up enough money, I would then find an apartment and live my life to the fullest.

Now we stood at the station once again, with just a suitcase and a few boxes of essentials to get me started.

"Sweetie," Mommy began, "I just wanted to say that I'm proud of your strength. Not a lot of girls, or even women, would strike out the way you did and continue on. You're my shero!" She looked at me with her big, beautiful eyes. I easily believed her. One thing Mommy was good at was encouragement.

"Aw, thank you, Mommy. That means a lot to me. But I'm not a shero—you are! I just did what I felt I needed to do to get out of there, to get us away from there."

My eyes teared up as we sat down on a bench. I had only about twenty or thirty minutes left to wait for the bus. The ride would be about fifteen hours long and I was going to enjoy every minute of it.

We sat there and chatted about our usual things: how I would decorate my apartment when I found a suitable one, how I would explore the city like a tourist, how Mommy would save her money and come visit me when I got settled—and before I knew it, they announced that my bus had arrived. We walked over to the line, and I took a deep breath, aware I was standing at the threshold of something new once more.

"Sweetie, I'm praying for your traveling mercies." She was smiling, but the look on her face didn't seem settled. I was leaving her again and she looked as if she was trying to keep it all together. My heart sank for a moment. Suddenly, I wondered if leaving her was the best thing.

I gave her a big hug. "Mommy, I'll be okay, I promise."

"Okay, sweetie. If it doesn't work out, just know you always have a home with me." She wiped the tears from both of our faces.

I picked up my things and the snacks that she had prepared for me and I hopped on the bus. I easily found a seat next to the window and waved to her as we pulled out and turned the corner. I looked until I could no longer see the bus station. It was harder than I thought to leave Mommy standing there, but I felt like I needed to do it.

Atlanta, for better and for worse, had been a growing experience. I was ashamed of how things had run their course, but, as the bus traveled down the highway, I was now going to leave it all behind me. I felt like going to Baltimore was how I could redeem myself. I was a locust shedding her skin. A new life awaited me and I was determined to live it! My butterflies began to wake up inside of me, and a smile crept across my face. I pressed my forehead against the cool window and looked out into the orange sunset. It was cold outside, but my heart was full and that was good enough for me.

At All Costs

Upon arriving in Baltimore, I woke up in time to catch a glimpse of the scenery. I could tell that this was a port city because of the waterways and loading docks I'd noticed along the highway. Although there were a lot of buildings, I was shocked at how old everything looked. I wasn't sure what I had been expecting, but I knew this was certainly going to be another adventure.

This relocation was different in that the people who were expecting me were of good character. The manager and his live-in girlfriend had arrived several weeks before me, so we would be connecting once I settled in. After I collected my belongings, I went outside to find a cab and the first thing I noticed was that it was really cold compared to Atlanta. There was even snow on the ground, which I could see had been trampled by foot and wheel to an ashen grey. I could hear the compacted snow, mingled with ice, crunch under the wheels of the vehicles passing on the street. The smell in the air was crisp and somewhat industrial.

Everything felt different and fresh, cleaner somehow.

I hailed a taxi and used the drive to take in as much of the city as I could. We zoomed by countless neighborhoods within the inner city. What impressed me the most were the row houses, which were five or six homes attached together in a row. After we exited the highway and took side streets, the row houses gave way to the suburbs. Although these neighborhood homes were older, they maintained a charm with their simplicity and sometimes manicured yards. Eventually, we pulled up to a two-story house. After paying my fare, I got my things and then mustered the courage to walk up and ring the doorbell.

Nervously waiting (I'd never rented a room to live in!), I began to wonder if anyone was home.

I was about to ring again when I suddenly heard a man say, "Hold on."

The inner door opened to reveal a middle-aged white man. Opening the screen door, he asked, "Are you Keeya?"

"Yes, I am," I said.

"Well, come on in, then. I'm Kent." He shuffled over to make room for me. "Yes, sir," I answered politely.

He showed me around the communal kitchen and then took me to my quarters, which were down in the basement. I was impressed at how spacious the room was. There was a queen-size bed, a table and chair by a small window, a love seat, and a bathroom. There was a TV and even a mini kitchen, complete with a microwave and a few hot plates for cooking. He then showed me the attic, where another tenant lived, and the washer and dryer.

"Well, there you have it," he said, giving me the keys. "Is this going to be okay for you?" "Yes, sir, it is." I was more than satisfied.

"Rent is due every two weeks. Just let me know if this is ever a problem. You have to buy your own food, and we don't allow loud music—you can go to the club for that."

"Yes, sir, that won't be a problem."

"Other than that, we stay to ourselves. Oh, and you're the only female, so if you ever feel uncomfortable, be sure to let me know, all right? I won't tolerate anyone being disrespectful to you."

"Yes, sir, I will. Thank you!"

As I got to know him a little bit, Kent struck me as someone who had been in the military. He looked like he was in his fifties, of a medium build, and a little under six feet. He was always firm in speech but kind. I didn't see him much, though. And I rarely saw the other guys since they were working all the time; the most we exchanged were morning greetings.

I liked my living space. I felt like I had been transported to the early '80s by the floor model Zenith color TV and the floral pattern on the bed. But what I liked best was the freedom and personal space the room provided me. It was cozy, private. It was affordable, too, which made it possible for me to save up my money and find a new place to live.

Baltimore was cold. It reminded me of the time our family lived in Ohio. When it snowed, we would make snow angels and snowmen with the neighborhood kids. We'd be out there for what seemed like hours. Only hunger or frostbite would bring us in for the day. Oh, yeah, we would have snowball fights, too, and if I got hit enough times in the face by a stray or well-targeted snowball, I might run home crying so Mommy could kiss me and get me warm again.

I also didn't have my own transportation in Baltimore, so I rode the bus everywhere. It was a daily adventure that I looked forward to. I felt so normal hopping off the bus and heading to the Inner Harbor to clock in for my shift. The bus dropped me off right at the front entrance.

As I walked across the small bridge, there were often tourists for whom I would take their pictures.

By the time summer came, I had saved up enough money to move into a small studio apartment closer to the harbor. The apartment was in a high-rise, overlooking Johns Hopkins University on the corner of 33rd and Charles Streets. The view, which stretched across the campus, was breathtaking. There were also two windows that opened up. Living on the seventh floor, I never got too close to the windows because I was afraid of heights. I often wondered if falling out of the window could happen by accident, my stomach queasy just at the thought of it.

I was happy to live in such a quaint urban area. My neighbors were mostly students and others like me who simply liked the area. There was a pub below, where, over the weekends, I could hear the loud, drunken people, mostly men getting into arguments or yelling across the street to one another. I steered clear of that place. I also observed a lot of the guys from various fraternities loitering about, their eyes wide with liquor and mayhem waiting to happen. One of the frat houses was farther down 33rd before you got to St. Paul Street. It seemed like those guys were always drunk. I wondered if they ever got any schoolwork done, or if their parents had a clue about their behavior at school. In contrast, Charles Street was lined with eateries, apartments, and various businesses leading into the downtown area. The hustle and bustle of this city was exciting to say the least.

I worked hard at Lefty's, but no matter how dedicated I was, it seemed the money wasn't enough. Despite this, I began making friends and connections here and there. The one who stood out the most was Angel, who managed a cart business across from me. We would often watch each other's store while one of us ran to the food court or the restroom. A lot of the conversations we had were about living on our own and having freedom from our parents. I learned she was about to graduate high school. Angel thought I was very bold to move out at such a young age. We laughed at so many things and quickly became good friends.

Before long, we decided to get an apartment together. It would help me get my finances in order, and it would help her to spread her wings. Angel was my first real roommate. We had more fun than we knew what to do with. This went on for months—until she got involved in a serious relationship. We often spent time with her family, but everywhere we would go, her boyfriend tagged along. He began to visit so much that it felt like he lived there, and this became a big problem between us. Eventually, as fate would have it, she became pregnant and moved back home suddenly.

Because Angel was gone, I couldn't afford the apartment with one job, so I grabbed additional work as a part-time hostess at the Baltimore Chart House at the Inner Harbor. I loved this job, not only because it helped pay some rent but because it was fun meeting tourists. Also, I was good at my job, I always wore a smile, and I got great tips.

The food was amazing and the employees were the best.

One of the guys I worked with was called Spanky. I mostly hung out with him because he was very friendly and funny, a great antidote for my loneliness. The only conversation I remember having with him was when he brought up how I could make more money than I was currently. This got my attention. Money was exactly what I felt would make my life better. I was tired of working two jobs and still not having enough to pay the bills. He had my ear.

"Keeya, what do you think about stripping?"

I began to laugh uncontrollably. "What? You're crazy."

"Yeah, you say that," he said, brushing off my skepticism, "but I know girls bringin' in a grand over a weekend. You'd be good at it, too. You're pretty, so you would make bank."

I immediately thought about the miniskirt contests I won back in Atlanta. This couldn't be that much different, could it?

"Yeah, Spanky, we'll see. I do need the money, but I don't know how to go about doing that."

"Well, don't complain to me about being broke," he answered with a shrug. "I already told you what to do if you need some cash. Just think of it like this: make enough money to get ahead on your bills and get out."

His words stayed with me over the next few weeks. During this time, I received an eviction notice, but fortunately I had already lined up my next apartment closer to Pratt Street, near the Baltimore Orioles' ballpark. It was a quaint little studio situated in a group of row houses that had been converted into apartments. Because of the remodeling, the layout had a quirkiness to it that I really liked. Walking into the apartment, you found there were sealed-off entrances that still had the crown molding to suggest a door used to be there or maybe a parlor in years past.

Still, I was determined to make life a little better at all costs. I ached over the idea of becoming a stripper. I liked my normal life, but I hated not ever having enough money.

Eventually, I convinced myself that my decision wasn't the end of the world. Just make enough and then get out, that's what Spanky had said. Right, I could do that.

A few weeks passed and by then I was pretty much settled into my new apartment. Once this was taken care of, I knew what came next. I waited until it was dark enough until the streetlights flickered on one by one. I walked to the El Dorado Lounge, which was a few streets down from my place.

It was a rainy night, so I wore a tan London Fog trench coat I had picked up from a thrift store and some rain boots. As I drew nearer, I hesitated. My mind raced with thoughts, and I wrestled with how this was going to work out. I glanced down at my boots, watching the slick rain slide right off and puddle onto the pavement below.

All of the progress I had made to live my normal life was now on the line. I sucked my emotions in, swallowed the lump in my throat, and reassured myself that this would be temporary and that no one would ever really know. I felt the sting of the lie I had just told myself.

It felt more like I was being convinced to sell my soul. A tear escaped from my eye.

Something inside of me felt like this was going to be difficult.

With each step I took, it was as if I felt the shame of my past walking with me, a feeling that became overwhelming. As I reached the front door, I could already hear the music blaring from inside.

I stopped.

What if I don't do this? What if I just turn around and find some other kind of employment? This isn't the only option, is it? I—

My thoughts were interrupted when a man came up and opened the door. He asked if I was coming in.

I looked at him and nodded yes.

The Wire

Because I was new, I made a ton of money. At the end of the first night, I was tired and hungry, but excited. I don't know how many drinks I'd had, but I called a cab to take me to a drive-thru and to my apartment nearby. When I got home, I stumbled down the hallway, fumbled for my keys, entered the room, and slammed the door behind me. My eyes focused long enough to count over four hundred dollars. At this rate, I could pay off my debts in weeks!

As I redeveloped my drinking habit, I soon picked up smoking weed again as well. Each vice, though, was my way of escaping what I was really doing. I tried to make every day a party. I tried to convince myself that this new way of life was better for me than suffering to pay bills and eat. And although I never felt in my heart that I fit in with this wild crowd, I kept forcing it.

I was reminded of the cheapness of my secret life each time I had to hide it from Mommy, whether in person or through the phone. I'd only seen her once since I'd moved to Baltimore and that was while I was working at the Chart House. There was no real need to update her about recent events. I didn't want to break her heart. With all of the money I received, I was cautious about giving her things—nothing too expensive or plentiful—because I didn't want her to figure it out. But while I knew she needed some of the money I was making, I became increasingly selfish, choosing instead to hide everything from her rather than support her financially.

My fun-and-party life also got thwarted by my internal struggle for significance. I hated myself for my choices, but I continued living this way because I wasn't sure if I could go back to working for just-over minimum wage. I had become addicted to the lifestyle, to the financial bounty I received. I also wanted to be beautiful, I wanted someone to need me. And I was wanted, even if it was only in the basest and most degrading ways. It was all so twisted. The more I lived this way, the more contrived my smiles were, and the less I knew who I was and for what purpose I was placed on this earth.

I began to hate myself and the men I kept company with. Didn't they have wives, daughters, nieces? It didn't seem to matter—to them or to me. I couldn't handle the loneliness I felt, and I was constantly reminded that I was far too perverted in my choices—past and present—to have any healthy relationship. Alanis Morissette's song, "You Oughta Know", was my painful reality. The anger she spewed out voiced the hurt coursing through my veins:

And I'm here to remind you, Of the mess you made When you went away.

Every guitar riff and drum roll agreed with the pain her words etched into my belief system. I was broken, beyond repair, hopelessly scuffling by. I did it with a smile and my face made up—a face that hid the despair of being a bottom feeder in an industry that couldn't care less.

This industry isn't about morality in the slightest, but about lust, power, and greed, all of which lay behind a smiling mask of entertainment and false autonomy. It produces a never-ending cycle of depravity, and not for just the patrons. I didn't want to admit just how greedy I'd become, for example. With the money I received, I bought myself leather coats and gold jewelry and even a diamond ring, just to feel important, but all those things couldn't satisfy the growing anger and resentment in my heart. I found I was turning colder with each passing day, lashing out at guys and even the fellow girls I'd formed friendships with. I grew tired of the sacrificial exchange of self for profit. My life was a big mess. I had a million ways to get a man to spend his money, but I couldn't find one way to have peace. Like a bird on a wire, I was free, but like a worm on a hook, I was trapped in this street life with no hope of release.

The El Dorado Lounge was a club with an infamous manager, whom I knew as Kevin.

He was a person of interest, so various law enforcement agencies had their eyes on the happenings of all who frequented his establishment. He knew how much he was being watched, so doped-up behavior from the dancers wasn't tolerated. While Kevin was usually very nice to us, if he felt someone was on drugs like heroin or cocaine, he quickly became a beast.

Because of his intensity, I feared him and made it my business to greet and humor him, making sure to steer clear of drugs while I was on the job. We had very light-hearted interactions. Occasionally, he would buy me some expensive drink to pay off my nightly dues, which always surprised me since I wasn't in his league at all. He never made a pass at me or grabbed me like property. He was always business-like.

Kevin reminded me of Mommy's stepfather. Both wore expensive hats and clothes like businessmen, had neatly trimmed mustaches, and projected authoritative airs so you always knew who was in charge. Kevin was like a modern black Godfather. The only thing missing was his ring being kissed by patrons. He knew the players, the pimps, the lawmakers. His intriguing connections extended further than I'd ever know.

One day, a group of guys came into the club. One of my dancer friends came over and told me who they were, explaining they were looking to buy out six girls to go to New York to be hostesses for a party over the weekend. We would receive $1,000 each, and our expenses would be paid. Girls who knew them vouched that we would be safe and come back in one piece because the guys had worked other parties like this in the past. We were told that there would be celebrities, but the event was not going to be raunchy at all—we would merely be part of the wait staff. Having done business with Kevin previously, this group easily received his blessing and selected six girls, including me.

At the news, we were so excited and I felt honored to be a part of such fun. It was going to be epic indeed!

We clocked out once our shifts ended and went shopping for clothes for the party. After we finished, we loaded up in a couple of the girls' SUVs and drove to New York, which was only a few hours away. We arrived at the Marriott Marquis off of Broadway. After we checked in, we were told we would be picked up later that night. While getting ready in our suite, we ate just about all of the snacks and ordered room service for drinks and more food.

The phone rang: it was time to head downstairs. Glitzy and glamorous, we were an impressive-looking group, turning heads as we entered the lobby. A tall, dark-skinned guy came forward, introducing himself as Slim before he directed us to four, brand-new black-on-black SUVs that were waiting for us. I could hear hip-hop blasting from the car speakers. Wanting to bop to the thudding beat, I felt like a celebrity.

On the way to our destination, I asked the driver (who was constantly on his mobile phone) where we were headed. He said to New Jersey for the private celebrity basketball tournament party at DJ KayGee's house. I was astonished. I was such a fan of Naughty By Nature, which was a world-renowned hip-hop group, and their DJ was one of my favorites. This was truly going to be an unforgettable trip!

We drove into a gated subdivision that was immaculately manicured, pulling up to a stunning mini mansion located in a popular suburb. The tree-lined street, which curled its way to the fancy abode, looked like something out of a fairy tale. Our SUV caravan entered the driveway through a beautiful, gated entrance that opened after the lead driver spoke to someone through the intercom. With smiles gleaming across our faces, we exited the vehicles and were escorted past expensive cars, parked by valet staff, and into the main house. I felt like we were in a music video montage.

The room we entered was on a lower level and appeared to be the game room, which expanded the length of the house. Everything you could think of was there for entertaining guests. There was a media room with a large projector and a screen that was motorized for whenever guests wanted to see a movie. There was a wet bar stocked with every adult beverage imaginable. The furniture looked custom-made by the way it fit into the unique spaces, the colors cleverly coordinated by an interior designer. From our vantage point, we could see this lower level contained several additional rooms. The place was all so spacious and expensive-looking. This mini mansion was massive, at least three stories.

Beyond the house were hills and a full-sized basketball court that was fenced in. There was a winding swimming pool and a huge deck that surrounded the back of the perimeter. In the distance, there was also a pool house. Toward the driveway and detached from the mansion was a two-story guest house, which also had a three-car garage, a kitchen, and a laundry area.

As we were given the tour, there were rooms that we could not go into, like the private recording studio or any room on the third floor. Taking everything in, we frequently *oohed* and *ahhed* our way around. Then, because the party would be starting soon, we were taken outside where wait staff had already begun setting up. We were told not to take pictures because most of the guests were celebrities and they had been invited to the host's personal home. We agreed and then learned what our duties would be: serve drinks for four hours, then we were free to mingle. Because there were so many people, the bartenders whipped up exotic drinks and filled our serving trays constantly.

Personally, I almost fainted as each person took drinks from my platter. Actors that I recognized but didn't know the names of. Queen Latifah. Mr. Dalvin from the group Jodeci. And the one that almost floored me was P. Diddy, complete with his entourage. I actually saw him exit his baby-blue Bentley (with a white interior) and I stopped and ran over to the edge of the deck to make sure I was seeing straight. It was unmistakably him. I ran back down to get more drinks and swiftly glided over to them to offer them drinks from my tray. I wish I could say he had something to say to me other than "Thank you," but he didn't.

I was still happy. By this time, the rest of the Naughty By Nature crew was there, Vinnie and Treach. What confused me was that, according to the magazines, Treach was supposed to be dating Pepa of Salt-N-Pepa, but here he was with OJ Simpson's daughter, Arnelle, and they were too close for comfort.

I kept serving refreshments as celebrities continued to mingle, occasionally sipping down ones for myself. I enjoyed every minute of this event—the food, the music, and, of course, the celebrity watching.

Everything was good until we were relieved of our duties and invited to come into the guest house to relax.
Slim looked over at me and asked, "So, what did you think?"

There were a few recognizable faces in the room, so I wanted to appear as in-the-know as possible. "It's a beautiful property," I answered confidently. "The event was nice."
He tilted his head and inquired, "So, are you ladies ready to make some real money?"

Honestly, I was exhausted and my feet were hurting from running up and down the stairs all night. I looked at the others, whose faces showed they were equally tired.

"What did you have in mind?" I asked, uncertain.

"Look over in the next room," he gestured. "Do you know who that is?"

We all turned our heads and one of the girls named Sunshine gasped. I knew my surprise had to be written plainly on my face.

Slim gave a deep and hearty laugh, calling me over to meet Mike Tyson, the womanizer and man known to beat up women. Yeah, the world may've considered him a heavyweight champion, but I knew his real reputation. I had no interest in him at all.

I took in the situation.

We'd been assured nothing sketchy was gonna happen. While we could clear some thousands of dollars, Tyson looked drunk or high. And there was no way I was going to do anything for him while he was in that state.

I shook my head no. I was afraid for myself and the girls, and the silent agreement was that we were not going to do it.

Slim, offended by my answer, came toward me; intimidated by his height and intense expression, I backed up closer to the door.

His voice was tight. "You mean we invited you here, paid all of your expenses, and you can't meet the heavyweight champion of the world? Do you know what you stand to gain and just how many women would give anything to be in your shoes right now?"

I froze. Something about his aggressiveness reminded me of Daddy and, without meaning to, I began to cry.

By now, all eyes were on our rising commotion. I heard someone mumble something, and Slim shoved us outside, following and yelling expletives. Additional derogatory comments were fired by Mike's entourage, but the verbal darts were cut off as the door closed behind Slim.

"Can someone just take us back to the hotel?" I asked, trying to sound braver than I felt.

In response, Slim pulled me by the arm and shook me violently, hissing, "You girls find your own way to the hotel!"

I didn't want to fight him because it was obvious that I would lose, and that made me cry more. When I screamed for him to let go, he pushed me away and I stumbled to regain my footing.

I was so embarrassed and upset as the reality that we were all alone sank in. We didn't know where we were, and it was a long way to walk in heels just to find a cab at 1 a.m.

The gates opened and we walked out. While I couldn't stop crying and asking myself what had just happened, the other girls argued back and forth about the situation. Some recanted and now wanted to stay and make the money, but others agreed with me. Since none of them no longer had a choice, though, we walked. With the solitary moon lighting our way, we walked for what seemed like an hour before we reached a main street. It took almost an additional forty-five minutes before we were able to flag down a cab that would take us back to the Marriott Marquis in New York.

Angry and exhausted, but relieved to be out of there, we rode back to the hotel in silence. I contemplated calling the cops or, better yet, the news station for what just went down.

But then I quickly realized it probably wasn't a good idea for either group to know where we worked. Kevin wouldn't like hearing about this, either—I knew he wouldn't want any newspapers or reporters coming to the club and giving him bad publicity. So, we decided to dismiss what had happened and to chalk it up as a bad experience.

I beat myself up thinking that I might have ruined it for everyone who had wanted the money. Some of them had kids, this could have been lucrative, what if he wasn't so bad after all? I thought about his divorce from Robin Givens, but what had been proposed just hadn't felt right. We were supposed to have had a clean night and, at the end, that wasn't what had been delivered. Standing up for myself and the others, though—that had felt good. For once, I knew I'd done the right thing. Feeling guilty, nonetheless, I apologized to the girls. Fortunately, they were mostly understanding. I think we were all just relieved that things didn't get any worse than they did.

Some find it hard to believe that a woman like me actually got sick of the lawlessness I frequently experienced and propagated. At times, I just wanted normalcy over money. A good, clean time over a loss of morality. Hmm. I guess I just wanted my cake and to eat it, too.

Chapter 15

Jagged-Edged Emotions

I was increasingly dissatisfied with my environment. Like with the miniskirt contests, the only thing that I liked about my work was having money every single night. The women I came in contact with on a daily basis were often just as miserable as me. Many of them had children they were raising from various relationships and saw this as the only way to pay the bills, while others were paying their way through college in hopes of a better life. Unfortunately, some girls had 'managers' who gave them very little of the profits they so desperately needed.

Fortunately, I wasn't bound to any day schedule like the others were. My morning and afternoon hours brought a somewhat soothing consolation to the night hours that I despised so much. I would spend these daytimes being a normal person who went shopping for clothes and household goods. I loved the fresh fish at Lexington Market and the clothing stores at Mondawmin Mall. I would occasionally find myself at the Inner Harbor for old times' sake, and I would run into someone I knew.

I often daydreamed of going to college and getting a degree in Journalism. I could tell a good story, a quality that came from hours of listening to Tony or to one of my favorite childhood radio programs like *Nightsounds*. Bill Pearce's voice was a frequent lullaby, deep and crystal clear. The questions he asked were often over my head, but he made me think deeply about life and its meaning. Or maybe I was inspired by *Adventures in Odyssey*, where the voice actors made Bible stories come alive week after week.

Eventually, I became close with one of the girls I worked with. I knew her as Kerry. She was one of the most level-headed girls there. She was a soon-to-be graduate of Morgan State University. Her favorite pastime was game show trivia, and she could answer over ninety percent of the questions on *Jeopardy* correctly.

Always transparent, Kerry appeared on a radio show with Kevin once, speaking very intelligently and boldly about the conditions of people like us. Of course, I had always found this ironic, since Kevin used the interview to advocate the One Million Man March, which promoted a healthier, unified African American society focused on fighting against economic and social ills plaguing our communities.

Kerry and I became roommates and moved to Towson, a suburb of Baltimore. I was glad we were together—I respected great thinkers and I had always wanted to be associated with someone who was smarter than the rest.

One Saturday night, we were driving home from another profitable time. It was icy outside from the previous snowstorm that week. We pulled into our apartment complex and slowly drove to our place. As we got out of the car, we saw a vehicle pull up nearby with the lights off. Four guys dressed in black with ski masks jumped out, one brandishing a gun, which he suddenly pointed right at me. At the sight of his weapon, I stopped dead in my tracks. Kerry, thinking quickly, tried to

run.

The man laughed, training his gun on my friend, and menacingly growled, "Don't even think about it."

When he had laughed, I noticed a diamond-encrusted fang grill on his teeth. My mind tried to place where I'd seen him before; something seemed familiar. But there was no time for that.
"Set your purses down, and nobody gets hurt," he commanded.

I did exactly what he said and motioned for Kerry to do the same. Crying, she threw her bag down. They cleared us out of at least eleven hundred dollars combined, not to mention the perfume, wallets, and our designer bags. Then, they jumped back into their car and drove off.

Immediately, we ran inside and cried. Thankfully, they hadn't forced us upstairs because things could've been a lot worse. I was grateful that we had our lives, that we could make more money and just buy new things. That night, our lives had been the biggest things at stake and we went home with those intact. Only later I would recognize who these thugs were—a fellow dancer's patrons, guys who hated us personally.

As my rocky life continued, I realized fear drove many of my decisions, affecting even my closest relationships as I viewed them with a negative mindset. By the time I reconnected with Mommy, for example, my mind was seared with pain. Although I loved her dearly, I regarded her with resentment. The dislike I held wasn't because she did something wrong to me, but because she didn't leave Daddy on her own—she had needed me for inspiration. Why hadn't she gotten herself out of that situation years ago?

But, in a strange way, I began to sort of understand why she stayed. My own experiences made me realize what a woman would go through to have a chance at a better life. In the moments when I endured the unthinkable, I related to her the most. It became more evident that she struggled and endured what she did in hopes that we would at least be able to have a family that was intact, fractured as it was.

Yes, it was warped thinking. Physical abuse does not make a healthy family nor is it conducive to healthy thinking, but Mommy didn't really have a support system of family and friends who could help her with her children. From the '70s to the mid-'90s, there weren't adequate programs available to offer social services and to help moms resettle. A mere thirty-day stay in a program for a physically and mentally battered woman with two children wasn't enough! These women also faced the overwhelming obstacle of unraveling the knots of self-doubt, self-deprecation, and physical threats before being able to access any real and permanent change.

My heart broke for Mommy because, for her whole life, she truly did the best she knew how with what she had to work with. Her health had always been a factor, and raising me and my brother had to have been difficult when we were constantly moving around. And it didn't help that my parents' relationship was strained and in and out of crisis all of the time. Their relationship was such a messy maze of unresolved emotions. I never got the impression that they loved each other, just that they were together. It's not that there weren't moments of joy and laughter, but those moments were overshadowed by the looming fear of a fallout between them.

It was difficult for me to grasp what it meant to have a loving relationship. In fact, all I'd ever experienced was a one-sided physical one, where I was faithful and the man was mine for the moment, but he wasn't anywhere near committed to me and my well-being as I was to him. Or even worse, there was nothing more than a physical relationship, filled with dates and time spent, that was often short-lived. I began to feel that I wasn't the type for real love and commitment. Even my female friendships followed this pattern, where I felt like a chick on the side—providing a listening ear, support, and a tangible presence, yet being recognized only half-heartedly or, even worse, not at all!

In public, I was a fair-weather companion. In private, though, I craved others' adoration and reveled in any substandard acknowledgement I received. I was so desperate to be valued, but instead I found myself settling for the thrill-seeking, self-deprecating cycle of self-hatred through worldly attention. See me, notice me, love me. All I desired was recognition for something other than what I could provide, and all I received was less than what was desirable or even acceptable. It was my fault. I didn't know how to respect myself enough to say no and mean it. Somehow, I felt incapable of any other behavior.

I felt like there had to be more to life than what I was living, but I just couldn't seem to find my way. I remembered the times when I was in children's church. The Sunday school teacher would tell us that each of our lives had a purpose. But what was it? What was my purpose? I had no idea. Not the slightest clue.

As a result, depression became my most constant companion, always reminding me of my failures and my shame. I could count on this heavy feeling going everywhere with me, a shadow that traveled with me every day of my life. It seemed the more I lived, the more I shed my concern for life. I became more and more comfortable even around guys who were known killers. I didn't know all of their names but that wasn't important. All that mattered was that they would come and pay me.

I even fantasized about dying, although I was afraid to really do it. It was a weird place to be. I knew one day I would make the attempt; with each fantasy, I was one step closer to becoming friends with the idea. I could never seem to drink enough or get high enough to silence the conflict inside my head. When I was drunk or high, the crazy world I lived in seemed to make sense. Under these influences, I actually found myself writing great poetry, expressions of glass-delicate thoughts and jagged-edged emotions. I had grown accustomed to dysfunction and every other happening in the underbelly of society.
I wasn't afraid of these people. I was one of them.

I was reminded of my naivety and the fragility of life whenever I received the too-often news that someone I knew had been sent to jail or shot and killed. Such consequences impressed upon me the truth that such a lifestyle was fast, furious, and terribly fleeting. The numbing reports I heard about my personal clients or people I worked with caused me to become so disillusioned with reality. Because of this, I decided that I had spent enough time in Maryland and began going to D. C. and New York to look there for nightly employment. Making money came easy as I traveled between different cities.

Eventually, I started a relationship with a guy from the Bronx in New York, yet another rocky, short-lived attempt at love when I really had only needed a place to crash when I was in town dancing. When I learned I was pregnant, my life was halted long enough to send me into another downward spiral of depression. I knew there was no future with this guy. He wasn't affluent, just a struggling singer in a music group with a well-known producer, but they were obscure in the industry at best. He didn't treat me wrong, but I knew he didn't love me. The decision was now a no-brainer. I could not—should not—have a child with him. So, I made the decision to have my final 'procedure'.

In addition to everything else going on, this particular avenue of abortion had become such a terrible path to trod. Sleep around, get pregnant, terminate. How could I have become so hard-hearted? While I was tormented by dreams of children, my actions demonstrated otherwise. I marveled at how routine this way of life had become for me. To me, this conditioning was the biggest failure of my morality. As far as I was concerned, I was a heartless murderer, selfish in every way.

I knew I needed help and that I couldn't continue to live this way. But how would I make the changes, and who would help me?

I made the choice to leave Baltimore and move back to Atlanta. There was just something about being near Mommy that was comforting. I didn't tell her about the pregnancy. I just moved in with her, had the abortion, and kept things quiet. While it wasn't long before I began my old habits, things weren't the same. In fact, they seemed to have intensified. I was deeper in the throes of depression than ever before. I lost about twenty pounds. I was a frail one-hundred-and-fifteen pounds and, being just three inches over five feet, it was noticeable. People began to ask if I was sick, but I would just say I was fine.

The truth was that I regretted my entire life! I was convinced that my existence was a mistake that never should have happened. I was plagued by nightmares of Daddy being angry with me, and I felt as if all children hated me. I couldn't watch movies that had loving father-daughter relationships without uncontrollable tears. And when I'd see kids with their parents around town, I would tear up. They seemed happy most of the time, and even when they were crying, they seemed so normal. I became jealous of people who appeared to be happy because they were enjoying something that seemed out of my reach. I wanted children, but I had convinced myself that I would never be good enough to be a mother, much less a wife. I was far beyond repair in my mind.

Regret became my middle name. During this time, I lived a somewhat reclusive life, choosing not to socialize with others. I stopped going to nightclubs to party, but I continued stripping by taking up work at Magic City. Mommy didn't know what to do with me. She knew something was wrong, but I was so distant with her, choosing instead to lie and say I was going to hang out with friends. Before long, I moved into my own apartment again.

Regardless, I still found a way to get myself into trouble.

One night after getting off work, I decided to get in a long line for a nearby street vendor, who was selling bootleg movies. There were two customers in front of me who I recognized as patrons from the club. The men turned around and spoke inappropriately to me. You might think someone in my position would be okay with rudeness, and maybe on another day I would have been, but I simply couldn't let this one go. After they turned away, I sharply insulted them right back and, before long, we were arguing. Ticked off, I stepped to the side to let people behind me continue in the line—I wasn't in the mood for movies anyway. Next thing I knew, one of the guys struck me and I fell to the ground. Then they were both beating me, punches and kicks, and then one of them pulled a gun out and pointed it at me.

Although my body ached with the pain they had inflicted, my eyes were fixed tensely on the shiny black weapon. Suddenly, sirens punctured the air, causing the guy to become nervous and put his gun up. They both fled the scene.

Watching the squad cars zoom up, I quickly realized the cops who whizzed by were not coming to my rescue but were continuing down the street and around the bend. Had it not been for their sirens, I might have lost my life at that moment. It could've only been God saving me.

Meanwhile, the crowd, mostly men, had just watched the whole thing and had done nothing to help. Finally, someone had the smarts to get the club's security.

As I was gathering my things, dazed from the fray, the off-duty officers escorted me to the basement office to ask me what happened—and they weren't kind about it. I felt like I was being treated as if I was the problem. One security guard grabbed my arm and practically dragged me into the building and down the stairs. Could he not tell *I* was the one who had been beaten up?

I argued and tried to explain that I was the one who was attacked, but he insisted that I had started the fight. I didn't think a young woman fighting two grown men was considered fair, so I became even more irate, which led to a scuffle with the officer. In the chaos, I kicked the security guard in the neck, and cops were called to the scene.

I was in big trouble now.

I made one last attempt to explain myself, but to no avail. When the cops arrived, it became obvious the two groups knew each other, and it was clear to me no justice would be served. I was booked for simple battery because of my behavior with the security guard. As it turns out, he and I knew each other. I had turned down his advances while I worked there. I had no interest in him, so maybe he was getting back at me by showing me what little power I had. Maybe I shouldn't have kicked him, but it wouldn't have changed the facts that sorely remained.

I was not worthy of protection.

I was a disturbance to the flow of business. I was the trash that had to be taken out.

Because of that horrible night, I became so aware of how little my life or safety mattered to others. In this world of sin, I was at the bottom rung. Based on the disrespect I'd received and the anger fuming inside of me, I knew I was in for a long night.

After being fingerprinted and having my mugshot taken, I was sent to wait in the processing area on the women's side, which was opposite the men's side. The guard overseeing us warned us women not to communicate with the men and vice versa.

Unfortunately, some idiot across the room kept yelling at me. Knowing where insults had gotten me last time, I chose to ignore him—not that it helped in the end. The guard felt like I was disrespecting his warning by somehow disturbing the peace, so he called for his subordinates to forcefully remove me. I couldn't understand why, once again, I was the target. The man was calling me, not the other way around! As punishment, the guards beat me up and physically threw me in a holding cell.

Aching from the fighting and being manhandled, and even more frustrated than before, I decided that I had had enough of this lifestyle. If this was where all of my efforts landed me, I was finished with it all.

I was thoroughly exhausted, hurting, and alone. Brooding in exasperated silence, I refused to speak the remainder of the time until I was allowed to make my phone call; by now, it had to be well into the next day. There was only one person who would believe me, the only one I could depend on. The phone rang several times…and then she picked up.

"Mommy?"

"Hey, sweetie, how are you?" Her voice was hesitant, yet it was the most comforting thing I'd heard for hours.

"I'm not doing too well, Mommy," I hastily admitted. "I got in a fight last night."

"I figured something was wrong," she said after a moment. "You usually call me if you're not coming home."

"Yeah, I know. I need you to bail me out. Mommy, this wasn't my fault. I was attacked by two men and, well, it's a long story." I didn't try to hide the weariness in my voice. "Let's just say it hasn't been a great night."

"Say no more, I'll do what I can."

Her assurance was the only thing I had.

I sat there in solitary confinement and sang "Amazing Grace", feeling the lyrics permeate the negativity I felt soaked with. As my words echoed, I occasionally surveyed my surroundings. When I caught an aggressive guard's eye, I averted my gaze. I rocked back and forth, and tears began their somber paths to my cleft chin. While I slowly sang, they flowed onto my neck and seeped into my prison attire. The scene was like something out of a Lifetime movie where the battered heroine has a moment of clarity after hitting rock-bottom.

I felt despondent as I remembered my journey over the last seven years—so much had happened, so much that I never would've imagined when I was younger. I wondered how I could reclaim my long-gone innocence. I mourned for the young girl who felt she had had no other choice but to hurriedly grow up by trading her purity for shame. At this realization, I felt another piece of me peeling away, like that locust shedding her skin.

A part of me would remain in the Fulton County jail that night, just across the street from Magic City.

The guard called my name several times.

I had lost track of how long I'd been sitting in that cell, having felt like I'd not seen the outside world for ages. I wiped my face. Tears had softened my cheeks so much that, as I walked, the air tickled them. I felt my eyelids were swollen from the night and day of crying. I imagined that I looked quite a sight. My suspicion was confirmed when I was walked to the exit and I looked into Mommy's loving and concerned eyes.

She simply embraced me as the tears rolled down our cheeks. At last, after one hard, long night, I felt loved and protected.

Like a Moth to a Flame

Despite the decision I had made in that cell, it became apparent that this pattern of living would be harder to break than I first realized. To escape the life I'd built my world around, I continued to look for shelter and rescue in older men, people I wanted to run to whenever I felt threatened and overwhelmed by the chaos. I was aware of this cycle and at times strove to free myself from it, only for me to enslave myself to it once more. You could say that I was making an attempt to replace Daddy and find love in one warped affair after another. This usually landed me in a predictable world of trouble, a trademark that I'd adopted since my first boyfriend. The game's path was old and well-worn, and the results were knowingly fleeting. No respectable man would ever entertain this type of relationship and neither would a respectable woman. Back then, though, I wasn't thinking about respect but of perceived survival. Initially, the survival was real, but after I came of age, it was a means to an end. Simply put, I hadn't fully realized and understood the alternate choices I had available to me. Most young women my age were in college and working toward securing a good job, and maybe a husband, too. I also wanted to be secure and productive, but how?

The only thing I blindly knew was to give the most sacred part of me away, over and over, for temporary acceptance. Rubbing shoulders with rich people or those who had access to money, legally or illegally, made me feel accomplished somehow. It was my twisted way of gaining some type of recognition. Oh, what a tangled web of disappointment I was stuck in. I seemed to only trust in my outward beauty and hang myself on the clearance rack. I wished there was someone who could have reached me to tell me I was worth more than I advertised myself for.

Then, at the age of twenty-two, I thought I'd met the person who was going to be my ticket to a new and fulfilling life.

One night while I was working at Magic City, I met a man who seemed to change the game. He was wearing all black and obviously knew his way around the gym. He was clean-shaven, and his smile looked as if he never missed a dental appointment. He was a tough guy or at least he appeared to be. He didn't ask a dance of me but to sit and talk with him, instead.

He looked at me intently as if taking in every single feature.

"I'm just in town working on a deal for a book and a movie I have in the works," he explained over the loud music and chatter.

"Oh, wow!" I exclaimed with raised eyebrows. My face must've been as brazen as my intentions. I pretended to be interested in his accomplishments. I couldn't care less about why he was in town, but there was something about him that was...magnetic, almost. "What's the book about?"

He merely smiled and put his head down as if debating something, then quickly looked at me. "I'm not sure if you could handle it, but it's deeply metaphysical."

I paused as I tried to figure out what he meant and, as if he was reading my mind, he chuckled, slightly apologetic. "I'd love to explain it in more detail, but it would take a long time."

I was so intrigued by what he was saying. This metaphysical business was new to me. He reached into his pocket and handed me his business card, but it wasn't like any card I'd ever seen before. The front was shiny and gold-brushed with *David Strong* engraved in metal; the back, in contrast, was silver-brushed and displayed the symbol of a circle and a pyramid intertwined, along with the words *Universal Metaphysics Council*.

At my puzzlement, David chuckled again. "We have a lot to talk about, I see."

Whatever he had to say, I wanted to hear. Never had I had a more intense encounter with someone before. I gave him my personal pager number and promised to keep in touch.

We spoke the next day for hours and continued to communicate through letters. He began to send me books on metaphysics, vibrations, and eastern pantheistic and monistic philosophies. I would devour the books and then ask for more, which he would send promptly. It was all so new and fascinating and different.

Whenever we talked, David spoke to me as if I was important. He never made me feel like he was looking to take anything away from me. I had to admit that no one had ever made me feel like he did. He often acknowledged my beauty but spent more time telling me that my mind was way more attractive to him. I couldn't get enough of being with him. Finally, I'd met the one who valued my mind over my body and desired me to be better, to rise above my station.

I began to visit him frequently in Elizabeth, New Jersey, where he was lived, and I realized as we began to grow closer that I was falling in love with him. Over the course of four months, though, he never tried to steal a kiss or suggest intimacy—something I found both refreshing and concerning. I finally asked if he was a down-low kind of guy. He assured me that he was and always had been straight, for which I was relieved. His respectfulness drew me in like a moth to a flame.

It was as if a spell had been cast on me. Never had I felt as if I needed to be around someone more than him, and never had I known a guy who wanted to take things slowly and considerately. I couldn't figure out why he hadn't made a move on me yet. We talked about it and he just said he didn't want to cheapen our relationship because I was too vulnerable. His answer surprised me. I wasn't familiar with being treasured.

As time passed, David suggested that I move to New Jersey and pursue a degree in Journalism at Rutgers University. With the latter being just what I had wanted, I gave his words serious consideration.

I thought I finally had met the man of my dreams.

If only I had listened to the warnings deep in my spirit.

During one of my visits, David revealed that he was a warlock aspiring to become a wizard. I was shocked at this news, but it didn't seem to matter to me. I knew his company consisted of bounty-hunting services, and I knew that he used metaphysical means to find fugitives. It didn't occur to me that he was utilizing black magic until his admission. Despite the alarm bells going off in my head, I remained hooked on him. What did it matter what he was into?

As our relationship continued, David took me around various parts of New Jersey. We ate in Hoboken, which was a cool area with lots of restaurants, and I enjoyed the most amazing Thai food and sticky rice ever. We shopped at little boutiques and even took the train to visit Manhattan and Greenwich Village.

After seeing some of the sights one time, we headed to a hotel room and settled in for the night. As we laughed and talked, David suddenly became serious and said that he needed to do something for me to help release me from my fears.

I was confused but went along with it. The next thing I knew, I was partaking in a satanic ritual. I noticed he wore an ankh around his neck, which gleamed in the light of the lamp. "This," he said, pulling it out so I could see it better, "I had energized in a river for you."

After this explanation, he had me turn the lamp off and kneel by the window, and then he pressed the amulet against my breastbone.

I literally felt a sensation enter my body through that ankh and I immediately became cold with fear. He had claimed I'd be released from my fears, but I felt as if the opposite had taken place. I looked around and felt an intense feeling of paranoia. The room felt darker, smaller even.

After this, he reassured me, "Now, you will never be alone again."

From that point on, I always sensed this dark presence with me, wherever I went. Sleep became next to impossible. I had been enchanted by David, but now I needed an explanation as to why I didn't feel safer with this enchantment. With unanswered questions, I returned to Atlanta. All the while, I felt a yearning to know how to combat this intense feeling of vulnerability I had in response to this *thing* that shadowed me. I needed an antidote to his spell. Something that would give me power instead.

Not thinking to call him in advance, I quickly booked an Amtrak ride back to Elizabeth. When I arrived, David was upset. He had asked me to move up there in the near future, but now he didn't seem too pleased with my sudden appearance.

"You're one who doesn't follow instructions." His voice had altered, reminding me of a sage from Middle Earth or something. Laughing with a strained lightheartedness, I retorted, "Tell me something I don't already know."

He gave no smile in response.

The days continued to pass, so I kept hounding him about when I could move into his house. His answer was that he was having repairs done to make it nice for me, which meant I would have to wait. In the meantime, I moved into a room one of his friends rented out near his place.

Impatient, one day I secretly followed him home, basically stalking him. I watched him drive to his house and park—and I stared open-mouthed as a woman and two children came out to greet him. My heart sank deeply. It all began to make sense. He was married!

Disappointed in David and angry at myself for getting

emotionally mixed up with him, a part of me cried, *Why does this always happen to me?*

I knew now that there would be no future with him, which I found to be an uncomfortably familiar feeling. Pretending I didn't know about his family, I continued to pressure him about the house and the move, wondering if he'd change his story that it was 'going to happen soon'. When he continued to lie, I eventually confronted him about his wife, which he denied, claiming they lived together as common law but were not married officially.

There was something wicked developing in my heart toward him. Not only him, but all men. From Daddy to everyone I'd met in between. The only man I felt a pure love for was my brother. Everyone else was wicked in my book.

I was upset with myself for moving to New Jersey. I had been so foolish yet again. As a result, I began to lose weight again and I became noticeably depressed. I would stay home all day, then go to dance at night. I had no friends to speak of.

Eventually, I met a guy who worked for a major hip-hop magazine, *XXL Magazine,* and he wanted me to write about my experiences in the dance industry. I was so excited—this was something I knew I could do well. It brought me back to the days of writing for *Dallas Weekly* when I was a teen. Inspired, I wrote a piece on the dance industry and how I wanted out. That article became one of many factors that encouraged my growing obsession to leave altogether.

When I later moved into a new apartment, I met a businessman who was interested in my desire to become a choreographer (a much more wholesome avenue for me, I might add). He was Paul Burgeon, a top executive for the Acapulco Black Film Festival. We talked and began to organize a troupe of ladies I would train for an upcoming pageant in New York. It was rumored that Debbie Allen, the famous dance choreographer, would be in the audience. Finally, I was going to do something Mommy would've been proud of.

A few weeks later, I interviewed in Burgeon's office. This office was the most elegant and sophisticated place I'd ever seen, demonstrating just how wealthy and influential this guy was. If this went well, it actually could be a big break for me. In his conference room, we watched videos of CeCe Winans and Halle Berry, raw footage that hadn't been edited yet. He asked me if I wanted a better life, so I shared with him the article that I wrote and how I'd moved to New Jersey to find out what else life had to offer. I had no idea what his intentions were, and I suspected I would be let down, but in the moment, I felt like I was made for more. I just didn't know how to get there. Before we could continue, his secretary called him away.

While I waited, I got up and walked over to the window. I leaned my head against the windowpane and took in the lovely New York skyline, twenty stories up.

And as I surveyed the landscape, I saw a shimmering golden stairway appear in midair. Literally, it had just come out of nowhere. Its shape reminded me of grand staircases in historic homes and old mansions. There were what appeared to be these translucent angelic beings ascending and descending the steps.
I stared, dumbfounded in disbelief. I immediately thought of Jacob's

ladder in the Bible.

That...wasn't what I was seeing, was it?

I began to feel somewhat unsettled by the apparition unfolding before my eyes.

Then I felt a hand touch my arm. Nearly jumping, I turned and saw it was Burgeon, who had reentered the room. When I looked back out the window, the vision had vanished.

Little did I realize, this brief phantasm would be only the beginning of many strange days ahead of me.

We ended our meeting and I went home.

As I arrived at my apartment, something felt off. I couldn't understand everything I'd experienced earlier in that office. I don't know if I was excited over the meeting or if I was confused about what I had seen out the window, or both. Despite having had an interview about a wonderful opportunity, I wasn't happy or content. My emotions were all over the place.

Something was *very* different, sad even.

I tried to relax, but I couldn't. I suddenly found myself thinking about my environment, where I lived. This apartment I lived in was the basement of a two-story house nestled in the quaint little neighborhood of Roselle Park. The landlords were a husband and wife with a school-aged little boy. The wife was pregnant and soon to deliver. One time, the husband came to my room, saying he just wanted to check on me. He invited me upstairs and I went, assuming his wife was there as well—maybe she needed me for something. When I noticed she wasn't in the house, I realized he was propositioning me. I didn't want any part of my very married landlord's nasty scheme.

My home was supposed to be the normal place in my life, my safe haven where I retreated from chaotic emotions and *those* kinds of pressures. It was my break from idiots like him. I never invited customers into this sacred space, and his proposition was too close for comfort. Did his wife know what type of trash she had for a husband, who would be so bold as to try something with his tenant who lived downstairs? I knew a change had to come quickly.

It also became more evident that my lifestyle was eroding all things decent within me. I lay in bed and considered ways I could become a normal person who didn't have to hide her lifestyle from her family.

Well, what might Mommy do to make this place lovely? I decided to go shopping to continue furnishing my little apartment. That was a baby step, at least. I enjoyed these moments, wishing I could walk into the stores with Mommy herself. I reminisced about the hours we spent talking about decorating and comparing ideas. Ever since I could remember, she and I would bring in and spray-paint a broken branch that we would hang on a blank wall, calling it art by God.

So, I did just that. I strolled down the street to the park, found the perfect branch, and dragged it home. I shopped a little in downtown Elizabeth and came home with spray paint and other knickknacks. I painted my feature wall terracotta, adding Egyptian papyrus in a floating glass frame. I then took the branch out back and sprayed it gold. I couldn't wait to see how it glimmered against the other decorations. Mommy would surely be impressed.

Thinking about Mommy made me miss her tremendously, so I decided to give her a call after a long night of dancing and morning of shopping and painting.

"Hi, Mommy," I greeted her. "How are you?"

"Oh, hi, Keeya! I'm doing good, just here figuring this pattern out."

Inwardly, I smiled. Mommy always found inspirational beauty in nature, which she used to create the most breathtaking environments for her clients. Curious, I asked, "What are you making now?"

"I decided to create a dress and I'm making my own pattern for it. It's going to have domain sleeves and a boat neckline."

"Oh, that sounds like it'll be pretty."

"Well, I hope so. You know, I'm tired of what they have in the stores for big women." "I know!"

"Every time I go into Lane Bryant, I just walk to the back of the store and walk out."

I waited a beat and then switched to another subject. "Mommy, have you heard from Tony?"

"Yes, I talked to him yesterday." "I miss him," I admitted.

"You should call him," she encouraged. "You know he'd love to hear your voice."

"So would I, but I really miss *seeing* him. I want to plan a visit. It's been way too long.

Mommy...do you think we could go and visit him? I know it's short notice, but I was thinking of going before the holidays. Like, in a few weeks, maybe?"

"I think that's a wonderful idea!" she exclaimed to my relief. "I can't remember the last time I saw my babies together. I know you're a grown woman, but you're still my baby!"

I smiled. "I know, Mommy."

"So, have you been able to register for school yet? You would make an excellent journalist. Your voice is so soothing, and you have great diction like me and your grandmother."

Oops. I had forgotten I'd told her that I wanted to register for Rutgers like me and David had talked about. I couldn't possibly tell her how my plan wasn't working out and that I wouldn't be registering for classes anytime soon. I didn't have the courage to find a GED class, much less take the exam.

Furthermore, Rutgers was clearly a pipe dream sold to me by David, my two-timing sugar daddy. I would have never followed him here had I known we were just going to be physical and nothing more. All of the times he shared with me about how he was waiting on his book to be released and how he could give people like me a helping hand was mere talk.

I took another deep breath.

"Mommy, I'm not sure when I'll be registering. I think I just need a break and to see you guys." My voice quivered and I tried to suck the emotions back in, but it was too late.

The tears began to stream as the weight of my deception gripped me by the throat. I was so *tired* of lying to them. In my heart, I really *did* want to go to Rutgers and become a journalist. But I simply felt I wasn't smart enough. I always looked like I was, but after Mommy took me out of public school and homeschooled me, I rebelled so hard that I didn't learn anything else after the sixth grade.

I was a sniffling mess now, which I knew could be heard over the line and Mommy, as she always did, came to my rescue.

"Keeya, I'll get a Greyhound bus ticket and meet you in Dallas. It's time for a reunion." Her voice was so calm and nurturing. All I wanted was to fall into her arms and cry. I knew she would not understand my tears, but she would sing her old songs and rock my pain away for the moment.

After we hung up the phone, I could hear the memory of her voice, singing in my ears,

When you walk through a storm, Hold your head up high,
And don't be afraid...

I couldn't remember the song to save my life, which frustrated me.

I stood up from the edge of the bed, grabbed my purse and some cash, and headed to the bar across the street. It was only about 4 p.m., but that was good enough for me. Sitting at the bar across from the regular customers, who looked even more pitiful than I did, I gave my double order of Old Grand-Dad and Coke. I drank it down, tipped the Spanish-looking bartender, and went back home. During the five-minute walk, with each step I felt the drink kick in.

Although I felt miserable that night after the alcohol, I was pleased that our reunion plans were coming together beautifully. I counted down the days in anticipation of the laughter and smiles we would all share.

When I finally flew into Dallas, Mommy and Tony met me at the arrivals area and baggage claim. They helped me get my things and Tony carried my bags to his trunk.

"Good to see you, Keeya," he greeted me. My brother never showed too much emotion, but his slight smile and tone of voice told me everything I needed to hear.

"You, too, Tony!" I couldn't keep my voice from beaming with excitement. With all of us together, I could easily imagine how Mommy felt.

On the drive out, I just couldn't keep quiet. Nobody could get a word in because I went on and on about how much I missed them.

Tony drove us to his new place in Pleasant Grove, which was

near Mesquite. I took in the sights since I had never been on that side of town before. We had always lived in North Dallas, so this was an adventure for me. We only had a couple of days there, but I was determined to enjoy this trip to the fullest.

Taking advantage that I had quieted down and gotten lost in the scenery, Mommy asked Tony her usual questions about his work and his wife.

We slowly pulled in the driveway, and Kendall opened the front door with a smile.

Although she and I had roughed each other up the last time we'd met, time had helped us smooth over the sharp edges of our relationship. And with everything I had been through, even *her* familiar face was enough to make my heart glad. She looked heavier than I remembered, but I grinned and jumped out to hug her just the same. I then looked past her and saw her younger sister and her nephew. We hurried in as Tony brought my things.

Sunday was one day I wouldn't soon forget.

That morning, I woke up nervous but excited, glad to be doing anything with my family.

We ate breakfast and headed to what Tony called a black megachurch. I listened to him talk about their pastor, who was a bishop. I didn't quite know what that was, but I figured he must be pretty important. What I was more excited about was going to church like old times with my family. It had been years since I'd stepped into one.

It seemed to take about half an hour to get there. We arrived in a long line of cars and we were soon guided skillfully by traffic attendants to a parking spot. I was in awe at how big the church was—I'd never seen a church so massive before. The services held at least seven thousand people at a time, so going there felt more like attending a conference. I learned there were also tons of classrooms and an activity building where youth services were held.

As we walked in, I kept looking down at my clothes, feeling self-conscious. I felt like my pants were too tight, that I was dressed too casually, and I wondered if Tony was okay with my appearance.

We were greeted by a beautiful older lady, with perfect milk-chocolate brown skin and well-coiffed honey-blonde hair twisted in a French roll style. "Welcome, welcome," she received us warmly, flashing the most contagious smile as she handed us each a program.

We stood in the lobby, talking until we were guided by ushers to take our seats. By sitting far back, we had a really great view of the pulpit.

With gospel music playing in the background, the atmosphere robust and filled with chattering voices, I looked around at the people pouring in. There had to be thousands of people here! I wondered if there would be enough seats for them.

Tony, who sat next to me, pushed my shoulder in his usual mischievous way, smiling playfully. I grinned. He did it a few more times until Mommy slapped his hand, causing us all to laugh.

A little bit later, someone got up on the stage and made announcements, and then the choir began to sing. I soaked it all in, but I found I was distracted by my feelings—everything was perfect, except Daddy wasn't there. We always went to church together when I was younger. Why would I be thinking of that right now?

The next song was a familiar one. The pastor stood up and swayed from side to side as the choir belted out the words I knew as a child. I began to be drawn into this song, and then I watched as people began to stand up and lift their hands in worship. I felt the need to join them, to stand up and be in the moment.

The pastor grabbed the mic after the song was over and began to hum and sing. He was a big man, but his voice was bigger. He sang from his heart, and I began to cry as I imagined Daddy singing. Daddy had such an amazing tenor voice.

I cried on and off through the entire service. I was convicted, conflicted, miserable, and happy all at once. Despite this, I ignored the altar call, though I knew I should've gone down. I felt glued to my seat by the emotional clashing inside.

The bishop's voice rang out like a large, tolling bell, his arms passionately outstretched toward the crowd as he roared, "*Backslider!* You *know* who you are! Come down to the altar and get right with God. He's waiting on you. You can only be blessed and have peace and sweet rest as you give Him your body and soul!"

I resisted the urge to run down the aisle even though so many others did. I felt my brother's eyes on me; when I glanced his way, he averted his gaze. Blocking him out, I cried deep tears. I couldn't figure out why I couldn't stop crying and then, before I knew it, the service was over.

We left the church and headed back to the house. I don't remember the ride back as much as I remember feeling more confused than ever. Our mini reunion ended the next morning as Mommy headed back to Atlanta and I returned to Elizabeth.

Something happened at that church. I couldn't articulate it, but it began to weigh heavily on me.

Chapter 17

How Do You Want It?

When I woke up for the third or fourth time, I looked around and realized I was in an unfamiliar setting. Although I was groggy, I immediately felt anxiety begin to build up somewhere between my chest and my throat. Thoughts began to emerge like a pale sun crawling out from behind a clouded horizon.

An assistant dressed in white came in with towels, which she set on the empty bed nearby and asked me, "Are you coming to breakfast today?"

I peered at her blankly and looked away.

I didn't want to speak to anyone. I didn't want to be here. She smiled at me politely and quietly left the room.

Alone, I gripped the edges of my bed in concentration. I kept trying to remember the details of how I ended up here, of how I got these scratches all over my body.

Just what had happened to me?

A woman's staticky voice crackled over the intercom, splintering my jagged thoughts: it was breakfast time.

I figured I'd get some answers if I ventured out of this room. I swiveled to the edge of the bed, put my feet on the cold, smooth floor, and stood dizzily. But by putting one foot in front of the other, I changed into the heather-grey sweatsuit waiting for me and trudged my way to breakfast. I took the first thing the cafeteria lady offered and found a seat in the corner, away from all of the strange, unfamiliar people.

As I was picking around at my cafeteria food, an older guy decided to sit next to me. His hair completely grey, he looked like a Columbian drug lord from the movies. He was slim and quiet, and surprisingly very neat in appearance. He greeted me mildly, but I could hear a deep accent. I wouldn't dare guess where he was really from, but I smiled mildly and stabbed at my food.

The entire time I was sitting there, I noticed a guy about my age nearby who kept looking at me. I tried to ignore him, but he, too, came over to see me.

Although I kept my head down, he commented, "So, you're eating today. That's good." There was a note of approval in his voice.

Puzzled, I looked up at him and realized that he knew something, remembered something that I didn't.
Exactly how long have I been in this place, anyway?

I recovered with a light reply, "Yes, I was hungry, so here I am."

He chuckled, obviously pleased, and said, "It's good to see you eating."

I was troubled by this interaction. Not because of this guy, but because my mind began to recall the events that led to my coming here...

After the reunion with my family, I recollect I rode back to my place in a daze, leaning my head against the cool window for support. Internally, I argued with myself about everything that had ever happened to me at the hands of a man, with David's mystical exploits and lie about having a family fresh in my mind. I wasn't in a good place, and after having returned to Elizabeth, there was a cloudy heaviness that weighed me down. Since the hour was late, I figured sleep was the best remedy for my restless mind and body.

The next day, I woke up thinking about my reunion with Tony and Mommy, a beautiful memory that made my heart smile and cry. I tried to go on with the day as normal, but normal evaded me. I went to the club as if under a haze and tried to work as usual, but something was different.

The pastor from my brother's church had said, "You're doing what you like but you no longer like what you do."

That's exactly what was happening. Drinking, for example, didn't seem to calm me down or have any real effect other than causing me to pass out if I had too much; it was no longer enjoyable. Nothing seemed to be. Over and over, the devil would ask me, *How do you want it?*
And over and over, I just couldn't to find pleasure in these empty attempts of living in the fast lane.

I called it an early night, hailed a cab, took in the familiar scenery, and ventured back into my little space to try and settle down. My routine was to count my money and place it in a shoe box. I had never bothered with a bank account because the shoe box was always open when I needed it.

I was unable to relax. I'd made enough money that night, but that wasn't the issue. My thoughts began to race vividly at warp speed. Several hours later, sleep still refused to weigh my eyelids down.

I turned the radio on to the usual Hot 97, hoping that would do the trick. I lit up a blunt that was from the other day. I got up and began dancing to the music. I finally exhausted myself and laid back down. I was dizzy, but alert, paranoid. Sleep finally came by daylight, and I stayed in bed all day long, taking cat naps. I had no desire to get out of bed, not even to brush my teeth or eat.

One thing was for sure: something was happening that I didn't like. I was spooking myself out at an alarming rate. If I could only keep myself from thinking so much. Better yet, if I could just get a decent night of sleep, I'd be just fine. At least I hoped so.

My evening routine somehow forced me out of bed. I showered, ate a little, and dressed for work. This night flew by like the others—I drank, I danced, I made money, I jumped in a cab.
When I arrived home, I unlocked the door and stepped over the threshold. Something felt strange.

I began to feel an insatiable urge to fix things, almost like a nesting mother preparing for her soon-to-be-born baby. I went on a mini rampage, tearing pages out of magazines that focused on world issues. I thought about all of the babies I didn't allow to live. As I taped several pictures of babies of different ethnicities up on the walls, their smiling faces blurred as tears poured from my eyes. When I stepped back to review my frenzied work, it looked like an eerie crime about to take place, like something out of a horror movie.

After turning on the radio and blaring music again, I busied myself going into every drawer and closet. I didn't know what I was looking for, but that didn't stop me from yanking every drawer out and flinging every door open and rummaging through the spaces looking for something, something, something.

In my feverish excitement, I felt something come over me. I don't know if it was the music, but I began to dance as if I was undergoing a ritual. I felt an evil presence enter the room—something was possessing me, I knew, but I was powerless to resist it.

In my small basement apartment, I found I liked the white, '50s-style refrigerator the best. Over time, I'd placed a pet tarantula in a small cage on the top of the fridge. Next to the cage, I'd put a Georgia peach candle, one of my favorite scents.
Compelled, I danced my way to the kitchen and lit the candle for its warm aroma.

Next, I picked up the cage and let my tarantula out, watching it crawl on my hand and up my arm. I felt it disappear from my shoulder and I became afraid, not knowing where it'd gone. It reappeared mischievously on my arm and I watched as the little creature slowly scuttled down into the palm of my hand. Its hairy body scurried lightly over my fingers and tickled my skin, and then it rolled onto its back. I knitted my brows, puzzled over this peculiar action. It had never done this before. Suddenly, its eight legs curled inward and stiffened.

Right in the palm of my hand, my pet tarantula had just inexplicably died!

Seeing the lit candle nearby, I numbly dropped the spider's frozen body on the tiny flame, which was instantly snuffed out by the arachnid's larger size. Seconds later, an acrid smell rose into the air.

I stared, stunned by what I had just done. Had I really just tried to set my dead pet on fire? What had I been thinking?

Before I could begin to feel remorse, a hard knocking jolted me out of this bewildered state. I threw my robe on and yelled through the door, "Who is it?"

"Your landlord," came a gruff reply.

I opened the door slowly, but the Haitian man rushed in, nearly barreling me over.

"What are you doing?" he demanded. Even with the music blasting, I could hear the hard edge in his words.

"Nothing," I stated, using the opportunity to switch the radio off.

"You lie." He found the source of the scorched odor and looked back at me. "In my country, this is how you start fires. You are inviting spirits to my home?" His expression seemed a mix of irritation and genuine fear.

At his words, I gasped and yelled defiantly, "Get out!"

He backed up in response to my anger, allowing me to slam the door in his face. I then went into my bedroom and crashed on the bed.

When I woke up, it was still the wee hours of the night. I felt an irresistible need to turn the radio on again. Sure enough, Hot 97 was still playing. *Little Kim's rapping again*, I thought dreamily. *She owns those airways...*

I passed out from exhaustion and woke up in the afternoon.

I headed to the local bar on the corner and drank myself silly, my usual response to the feeling of despair would seep into my daylight hours after I'd had a long, hard night. Stumbling, I headed back toward home.

Then, because a familiar car caught my eye, I roamed the neighborhood—I could have sworn that was David's vehicle circling the block...

Next thing I knew, it was the evening time, just before when the sun went down.

I had still been wandering the neighborhood, and I vaguely remember jumping in front of a car, trying to commit suicide; the driver, a kind, middle-aged white lady, had blocked traffic and called the police. Amid the glare of the headlights, I recall she had looked at me and had mouthed something like, *It will be okay.* Cars were honking their horns and their loud blasts hurt my ears. I sure didn't feel okay.

I fled the scene, running back home because I was afraid that I would be in trouble.

At the door, I was greeted by David, who looked very concerned, but there seemed to be a sinister edge to his expression. A part of me felt as if he had been watching me lose it all along. I could have sworn that I had glimpsed him driving at different times that night, as if he was spying on me.

I was also acutely aware that all of this could have been playing out in my head. I just couldn't seem to keep track of reality and fantasy. The lines had blurred, and there was no one to sort it all out for me. Was I beginning to go crazy?

David led me inside and sat down, pulling me onto his lap.

As I looked at him, though, his face seemed to morph into a very red, very aged face. It was horrific! It was like a moment in a sci-fi movie where the human would alter, revealing a gruesome alien.

Frightened by this transformation, I jumped out of his embrace as though I had been physically burned.

Then, as quickly as it had changed, his face returned to normal and he left me there, stunned.

Time seemed to stand still while I slid into a chair, disturbed by what I'd just witnessed. What in the world had just happened? Was what I had just seen really *real?* All I was aware of was how fast my heart was pounding in my chest and of my blood thudding against my temples. I shuddered.

After several minutes, I managed to shake myself out of my

stupor. I gathered my wits and wandered outside to look for David—only to be greeted by two of New Jersey's finest, one black cop and one white cop.

I'll never forget this day as long as I live! I laughed nervously to myself, feeling dizzy with disbelief.

I couldn't figure out why they were there. All I wanted to know was where David had gone, and these guys were distracting me from finding him. Besides, I didn't like cops. All the cops on Daddy's side of the family were crooked, the type that would beat up drug dealers for their money and their dope. I'd encountered officers who solicited my services while they were off duty when I was in Georgia, and there had been the ones who frisked me crudely instead of calling for a female officer when I got pulled over in New Jersey. So, what did I have to expect from these two?

They asked my name and where I lived.

I gave them my name and told them I was already at home.

As I answered their questions, I noticed the curtain move in an upstairs window above me. Maybe my landlord or his wife had called the cops on me.

The policemen told me several calls had come in about a woman running in the street, trying to get hit.

At their words, fear quickly gripped me. I knew I was in trouble. I put my head down and surrendered in tears.

I was that woman. I was out of control. I obviously couldn't help myself at this point.

The cops consoled me as they led me to a nearby bench, reassuring me that I wasn't in trouble and they would take me to get help. As they finished their questions, they appeared saddened by my situation. The white officer sat next to me and I collapsed on his shoulder. He comforted me as if I was his family. The black cop called for an ambulance.

Despite their kindness, a part of me remained guarded. What if it was all for show? They weren't going to rough me up in the end, were they? My expression must've given my thoughts away, because the white cop's eyes filled with tears and he walked away to collect himself; the black cop placed a small blanket around my shoulders. Their actions conquered my doubt and touched me deeply. Their concern—real concern—was the last thing I had expected, and I allowed myself to feel relief as they soothed me. Mommy always said not to judge anyone by the color of their skin but by their behavior toward others. It was obvious these two cops were providing a real service. I had never realized that they could bring comfort. I thought they just exacted punishment and abuse.

At the sound of the ambulance drawing near, I felt a fresh stream of tears flow from my eyes. As the medical vehicle drove up, my landlords looked out of the window, their blank expressions confirming that I was a poor, confused soul. Aware of their eyes on me, I hung my head as I was strapped into the gurney. During this process, the medical staff was so kind, taking care to speak softly. I was lifted up and inside the vehicle, and the doors closed behind me with a thud. Once I was inside the small enclosure, my vitals were taken, and we were off.

After we arrived at the hospital, I was whisked into an examination room. They transferred me to a cold bed and approached me with a needle, which made me nervous. Once I was injected, though, the dose of whatever they gave me changed the entire game. I began to hallucinate and twitch, my mind going off to another world entirely. *This stuff must...be what they gave the...writer of Alice in Wonderland...* I thought disconnectedly. I know I eventually succumbed to the trippy ride, but I have no memories of what I experienced.

Later, the effects of the drug wearing off, I woke up in a room that was similar to a hospital room but it was extremely bright. There was a window to my left and a bed that was empty. There was a single painting on the wall—the only spot color—which was a watercolor abstract.

As I gradually observed more of my surroundings, I noticed some papers on the nightstand. One of them listed 'activities' for the day and I was beginning to scan it when an assistant came into the room. She took my vitals and asked me how I was doing. She was so nice, but I couldn't bring myself to smile at her.

She let me know that the doctor was making her rounds and that she would be with me soon. As she was speaking, the door opened slowly and a small woman asked if she could come in.
I sat up in the bed and said yes.

"I'm Dr. Ho," she said, entering. "I would like to know how you are

feeling today." Somewhat unsure, I answered, "I'm okay, I guess."
She smiled and, with a soft, polite voice, asked, "Do you know why you're here?" "Kind of…"

She nodded and explained, "You were trying to hurt yourself, and a neighbor complained of a woman roaming the streets and jumping in front of cars." When she saw my alarmed expression, she confirmed, "Yes, you were running from house to house, and the police showed up at your door."
I looked down, ashamed.

Noting my response, Dr. Ho added, "We are going to help you and see what's going on with you, okay?"
"Okay," I whispered, pulling the covers on me as I slouched in the bed.

I noticed that she didn't have a single trace of an accent even though she was clearly of Asian descent. My mind tried to contrive a story as to where she came from, who her parents might be, and how she decided to become a doctor in a hospital in Elizabeth, New Jersey. I bored myself with stereotypical scenarios within only a few short moments.
As Dr. Ho left, the assistant handed me a piece of paper before leaving the room. It read:

David called at 9:34 a.m. 9/20/1997
202-555-1234

It was apparent that I had finally landed myself in the psych ward. I was being evaluated and there was nothing I could do about it.

Still, I had to figure out how to get out of here—and fast. These people had me all wrong. I needed help, just not in here!

And even with my addled brain, I knew David was the only person I wanted to speak with.

I found some socks to put on and I headed to the phone room. I had to hear his voice. I needed him (and answers) now more than ever. I dialed the number, but there was no answer. I tried again later, but got the same result. He knew I was here, so why wouldn't he pick up? Frustrated, I gave up and went back to my room.

The evaluation and diagnosis seemed to be more than I could handle: bipolar disorder.

I was shocked and embarrassed. I knew that I'd been through a lot, but I couldn't imagine living with this condition, much less telling someone that it was something I suffered with. What about the demonic spirits I'd encountered? Surely, they were partly to blame. The last thing I needed was to have one more thing to throw into my misfit kit. All I could think about was the forthcoming judgment that I would encounter from people. The idea made me feel sick.

And to top it off, David never returned my calls. What was he doing? Why wouldn't he call me back? And as it turns out, the number he left wasn't even a real number. He was deceiving me even with that. What type of person was he? How did I get into this mess?

Although the medicine I was given was successful in helping me maintain a semi-emotionless state, even to the point of making tears impossible, it couldn't suppress my thought life. Those continued to run rampant, even keeping me up at night. I continued to draw the same unhealthy conclusions as I did before, only they were more matter-of-fact. I found I was computing like the *Star Trek* character, Data. What a weird condition to find oneself in.

I thought the people around me were the crazy ones. Somehow, I was different, I didn't belong in this looney bin. The problem with the theory of the others being crazy, though, was that if they were the ones with the problem, then why was I here? Once I arrived at that consideration, I threw my sanity notion out the window. If I was here, then I was equally as crazy, disturbed, and hopeless, a mere lodger on the thirteenth floor of the Elizabeth Emergency Care Unit.

As I battled wakefulness night after night, just trying to fall asleep, I would relive all the hurtful and painful situations that led to the collapse of my mental state. The situations of abandonment beginning with my father. The sexually abusive situations I found myself in. The promiscuous escapades I endured as a perceived means to an end. The lawless associations that I was involved with. The lies I purported to escape judgment, only to be judged anyway. I was tormented with my life's choices. It didn't matter whether it was my fault or my parents' faults for failing to protect and guide my innocence. My condition was the evidence of what I felt was a wasted life.

Heck, even my death wishes had failed me. All the attempts I'd consciously made to be in the wrong place at the wrong time failed to kill me. Deep down, I was too afraid to carry out my own overt suicide. After all, I'd probably mess that up, too, and be the oddball who lived in some maimed, retarded state, somehow worse off than when I started. I had no faith in my ability to succeed at anything—not even suicide.

Now, to add mud to the water, I touted a psychological diagnosis to drive the nail deeper into my mentally incompetent coffin.
And the bipolar disorder wasn't the only thing I dealt with as I lived in the psych ward.

During my stay, I developed and experienced a number of conditions.

The most prominent was a terrible little persona that accompanied my state of psychosis—a messiah complex. Without warning, I would become the answer to everyone's problems that ever existed. I had delusions of preparing a speech that I would give to my royal subjects, for example. I couldn't seem to control when this would happen, and my voice would even change as I mentally switched over. It was as though I'd practiced for a play or movie, and I would argue with anyone who told me I was wrong. This would cause the staff to inject me with something so strong that I would pass out and wake up back in my bed.

Another annoyance I experienced was a type of escapism called mental regression, which often accompanied my responses to people. This was where, in my mind's hampered ability to cope with the breakdown that had occurred, I 'escaped' mentally into a childlike persona to avoid further mental damage.

Lastly, though understandably so, I dealt with a deep paranoia. Occasionally, I would hallucinate. I tried to keep this to myself as much as possible, not wanting to concern people any more than I had to. I knew I was a handful.

Talk about issues! I had so many to cope with now. It was overwhelming and left me feeling even more hopeless. As if my screwed-up life and the diagnosis weren't enough, there were all of these mentally crippling accoutrements now along for the ride.
I was officially a loser.

Despite all of this, something about my time on the loony bird floor captured the hearts of my mother and brother. When they would speak to me over the phone, they addressed me as though I was a child. I guess they didn't know how to approach me, not knowing how far gone I might be. Though to be fair, the conversations were often one-sided anyway because my thinking was sped up a mile a minute. And I'm not sure what words were coming out of my mouth whenever I did speak, but they were at an uncontrollable rate. I know I felt apologetic and knew something was terribly wrong, but I was unable to stop this progression, whatever it was. Our time together is hazy at best for me. I do remember experiencing moments of utter hopelessness, which were followed by feelings of grandiose importance (the messiah complex was probably to blame for that).

During my time there, I found I distrusted the clinical environment because it was filled with other tortured souls who were confined to the psych ward. There was no shortage of drooling individuals, clearly overmedicated, who stared blankly into Never Never Land. Yet while not everyone was rocking back and forth, and there were no baskets being weaved, the eyes of each person appeared dead, hopeless, pitiful. *What happened to them?* I would wonder. Some looked to be no more than teenagers, while others had completely white hair, people who obviously had never healed from their stories of tragedy and shame. I didn't want to relate to these people, yet here I was surrounded by them.

Sometimes, someone would scream out and the staff would drag him or her to a room for shock treatments, which were still utilized to treat bipolar disorder, schizophrenia, and severe clinical depression. The person underwent medically induced seizures to help ease the symptoms of their manic episode by use of electricity, a practice that had been around since the 1930s.
Horror movies featuring such practices, such as *One Flew Over the Cuckoo's Nest* with Jack Nicholson, would often come to mind. I could only imagine what terror that person had to be experiencing.

Witnessing that on a weekly basis, I made sure to be on my best behavior to avoid becoming *that* person, which meant I stayed in my room most of the time. The other reason I stayed in my room was that I hated being regarded as a psych patient by others. When I was by myself, I had less interaction with the frequent staff and unstable patients.

The visitation room, as a result, was one of the only two normal places. I remember it was decorated in mauve and federal blue patterns from the late '80s. From what I could see, Mommy certainly needed to help them out with their decorating—and everyone would be better for it. It was a sitting room that was around the corner from the nurse's station, with coffee and tea and a TV that was set on some news station. There was a series of color-coded entryways, where visitors were escorted in order to guard against the possibility of mayhem where the crazies hung out. The cafeteria, also, was the other place of normalcy, where well-behaved patients could come eat with visiting family members; the thick, locked doors at the end of every hallway leading to the cafeteria ensured no screams could be heard outside of the room.

    The only patient I cared to talk with was the Columbian-looking guy. I've always gravitated to people from other cultures. I guess it's the military brat in me. At mealtimes, this guy would always smile and speak to me like a normal person. He would always be humming one song or another.

    One day, I got the courage to ask him about a song they often played on the radio station. We had all just finished getting our cafeteria trays, and he was several people ahead of me. I saw him gather his condiments and I decided to sit wherever he did, which was usually alone.

I arrived at his table with my tray in hand, asking, "Can I sit here?" He glanced at me with a smile. "Sure," he answered and began eating. "Do you like music?" I asked, not sure how much English he spoke.

    "Yes, yes," he answered, looking up as if anticipating a conversation, his voice deep and colorful. He seemed like me: to be relieved that this spark of normalcy could exist in such an environment. In my usual friendly fashion, I asked him, "Do you know the song, "Guantanamera"?" He smiled again and now appeared curious.

With something the closest to joy that I'd felt since my arrival, I belted out the chorus:

Guantanamera,

Guajira Guantanamera. Guantanameeeeerrrraaaa, Guajira Guantanamera!

The man grinned in appreciation and said, "*Bueno*, that's a happy song." I smiled back, satisfied with my accomplishment.

Some people stared at me after my singing and some kept their heads down over their meals, but I didn't care. I was entitled to have a crazy moment. Worst things had happened to me, after all. I continued to pick at my food after that and then bit back a wide grin, aware the staff's eyes were watching me.

It was the first real outburst I could recall having since I arrived. I'm sure it was written in someone's report.

Whenever I spent time speaking with Dr. Ho, she would reveal yet another reason I was there. I don't know why I remember this, but the last conversation we had puzzled me.

"Keeya, what happened to bring you to this point? Do you know?" I sensed her genuine desire to learn more about me.

"Dr. Ho, were you there when I was born in Madrid, Spain?" I asked suddenly. "Because your eyes look familiar."

Her expression never revealed what she thought of the odd question. "Probably not," she answered, "but maybe it was another Asian lady who delivered you."

"Oh," I said. I sat in the bed with my chin propped on my knees, which I had drawn up to my chest.

"Were you aware that neighbors the night before called the police about a black lady running around the neighborhood completely nude?"

Embarrassed by her sudden words, I looked straight at the wall with its single piece of artwork. I gazed into the painted scene and tried to understand why the colors blurred into each other. Did the artist know that the painting would be in a place like this, being stared at by a woman like me? I sat there, wanting Dr. Ho to skip this part.

Recalling the details was surreal. I knew it had happened, although at the moment the event was somewhat vague in my mind because of the meds competing to gain control of my imbalances.

The night that I lost my mind, I was naked, crawling in a creek bed at the park near my rented basement. When I noticed the full moon above me, my body contorted in an unnatural way. I felt cursed, engulfed in a timeless void of physical pain and mental anguish. I knew that night had something to do with David, that I had been under a spell. And even here in the psych ward, I could still sense the spirit he'd had summoned from that hotel room shadowing my every move. I couldn't tell this doctor all of that. Then she would really be convinced of my craziness. I wanted out of here, so I wasn't going to give any details that would make matters worse.

"Keeya," Dr. Ho said gently, "you don't have to talk about this if you don't want to."

I realized my brow was deeply furrowed and my hands clenched my ankles. At her words, I felt relieved to shake the memory, yet paranoid that another piece of my messed-up life had been unearthed despite my attempt to bury it deep.

Internally, my heart wept (I couldn't cry anymore, remember?). Although the medicine calmed most of my knotted emotions, it was impossible to escape them all. The one emotion the medicine couldn't reach was the oppressive feeling I experienced now: utter embarrassment, coupled with hopelessness.

I stared ahead until Dr. Ho concluded her questions, got up, and left the room, followed by the medication aide. I took the scheduled dose that had been left for me and stared straight ahead at my only comfort in that cold room: the abstract painting.

I did have something to look forward to, though. Tony and his wife had said they would come and take me back to Dallas, to where they lived. The only thing I didn't look forward to was revealing everything that had landed me here. Through all of our conversations, I'd never mentioned why I was there in the first place. It mattered to me what Tony thought about me. I was terrified to confess everything I'd really been up to. I was sure the clinicians told him all of the readily important stuff anyway, and that was enough embarrassment to cause the tower of Pisa to lean.

I had made up my mind that having bipolar disorder was not what I wanted to be known for. It would not define me or my life. It was too unpredictable. It was something that made me feel out of control. It ruined my chances of being considered normal. I decided never to tell someone I had this diagnosis or mention any of the other conditions I was dealing with. They were like the mental scarlet letter I vowed to keep covered up.

But how?

Finally, the appointed day came. I was packed and ready to go, with something like a restlessness anxiety nestled in the pit of my stomach. Instead of the familiar butterflies, there a massive, lopsided ball of worms, squirming and vile. While I was relieved to be discharged, the eagerness I felt was overshadowed by fear. What if I couldn't stop acting like a crazy person? I felt the chip on my shoulder widen at the thought that someone would disapprove of me because of this dirty little diagnosis. What if any of the other conditions decided to rear their ugly heads? Although the meds kept me relatively stable, I still struggled with the paranoia and all that entailed. I didn't want to worry Tony and Kendall any more than I had to. After all, they had made the sacrifice to take me in. I would just have to keep quiet about it all at all costs as much as I could.

The attendant came to my room and told me that my family had arrived. I hurried to get my things in hand and followed them through the usually locked doors into a hallway, which led to an elevator.

We soon entered a room where Tony and Kendall were waiting and they greeted me with long hugs. Aware they knew how severe my loss of contact with reality was, I had no idea how they would respond. I could tell Tony's movements and speech were so calculated yet compassionate. The way he looked at me was so telling: he was devastated. Kendall, also, was compassionate and calm. I was most certainly 'damaged goods', but seeing their familiar faces brought me comfort, and that comfort was all I had to hold onto.

The lady who sat behind the desk seemed concerned for my well-being. She sat down and invited us to do the same. Before we signed the necessary documents to get me discharged, she explained the process of release and then stopped.

"Mr. Greene," she said, "please leave the address blank. You've mentioned that Keeya is being taken back to Texas with you and your wife. Am I right?" When he nodded, she continued, "Then allow me to fill in the address. I cannot allow the patient to be released to family who lives out-of-state. They're trying to commit her to the state hospital for further evaluation. Trust me, it won't be as simple to get her out of there as it is here."

"Understood."

Tony glanced at me and left the area blank.

The woman looked at me and tilted her head to one side. Her eyes were sincere and her voice was matter-of-fact. "Young lady, you don't belong here. Go home with your family."

Despite the medication in my body, I felt a tear escape my eye and stream down my unsuspecting cheek. Her words had brought humanity back to my downtrodden soul.

Chapter 18

Back to Life!

We left the hospital and headed back to my place to gather what we could of my things. David had been in communication with Tony and had arranged to meet me there. Although I was angry that he had cut ties with me, I felt David would provide a good explanation that would refute my doubts about him.

On the way there, my mind raced with which question I'd ask first. But when we met, David treated me as if I was someone he didn't know personally, intimately. He spoke more to Tony than to me, barely looking my way. It was as if he knew the details of my meltdown and now wanted nothing more to do with me.

It felt like I was being handed over to the authorities. This was merely a transaction.

I gathered enough clothing for the trip and didn't think to grab my most important possession in the world—my picture album. I told David that I would send for my things once I got settled and he agreed to keep them for me.

Just before hitting the road, Tony leaned over David's forest-green Toyota Land Rover and pulled out a twig that was lodged in the headlight. It was such a simple gesture, but it meant to me we were turning over a new leaf. I felt peace in heading home to Dallas with

Tony. Finally, I would be reunited with those who really loved me. I knew I had promised myself that I would never return to Dallas, but somehow that no longer mattered.

The journey back to Texas was a blur. The midnight sky is all I can really remember regarding the scenery. I recall I had random, disconnected thoughts, too, which I dared not share with my brother and sister-in-law. I was keenly aware of my mental state and didn't want to embarrass them. Although the medication I was sent home with was currently in my system, I could tell it wasn't as strong as what I'd had in the hospital.

When we arrived back in Dallas and got settled in, Tony made a few things very clear to me. "Keeya, I know you've been through a lot, but all of those strange books you have, we're getting rid of them."
I nodded and inside I knew things would be better somehow.

"Oh, and one more thing, Keeya. We're going to church like we used to when you were little."

At his words, I looked up from where I was sitting on the sofa. Glad we'd be going to church again, I smiled. "Okay, Tony."

While I lived at their place, Tony and Kendall had a dog that was so sweet. He was a tan chow named Baloo. Throughout the day, he was my biggest joy, becoming my unofficial therapy. I would feed him and over time I gained the responsibility of walking him. Eventually, Kendall returned to work, leaving me home alone with Baloo. All I did, day in and day out, was watch Christian television and play with Baloo.

Although the daytime was relatively peaceful, nighttime was a different story. As darkness fell, I would find myself battling an overwhelming sense of fear. As a result, falling asleep was the most difficult feat ever. Night after night, the fear I felt became stifling.

I'd attempt to fall asleep but to no avail. I would become too afraid to sleep in the room they'd prepared for me, so when I experienced these 'fright spells', I would sleep on the sofa in the living room, which was near their bedroom door. I would feel fear building up between my stomach and my throat. I knew that then, whenever I did fall asleep, I would have nightmares that felt so real that I would wake up sweating and crying. Someone was always chasing me to hurt or kill me.

One night, in the middle of one of these fear attacks, I was frightened by Baloo barking and panting. The sound of his wheezing became louder and, as he came closer, I covered my head with my blanket and wrapped myself up real tight. I wanted to call Tony, but I didn't want to wake them up. Instead, I rocked back and forth in the darkness, my eyes closed tightly as tears streamed down my face. Then I heard the panting huff in the living room and Baloo stopped in front of me.

A small part of my scared mind tried to comfort me, reassure me. This was Baloo, my friend! A fluff ball who had just wanted to see what was wrong. I wondered if stroking him would coax me out of my fearful state.

I gulped and exhaled shakily. *Ye-yeah, spending some time with him might help me calm down a bit.*

When I dared to remove the covers from my head, I saw nothing was there. No Baloo.

Just empty space.

And the gasping sounds.

I froze in icy fear as the disembodied breathing continued, which then gave way to noisy sounds of furious scampering and darting movements around the room—but I couldn't see *anything!*
Then I sensed another worldly, invisible presence in the room. It felt larger, more intense. And I knew in that moment that I was in terrible danger.
To combat these beings, I immediately began to pray like never before; it was the most honest prayer that I had ever offered. "Lord Jesus, if You are real, please save me! Cover me with Your blood, from the top of my head to the soles of my feet!" I don't know where that prayer came from, but I'd heard people at church long ago pray like that. Instantly, a third presence entered the room.

A warm liquid sensation coated my head and flowed down to my feet, covering my body.

As this presence enveloped me, I felt an overwhelming sense of peace wash over me.

Feeling nothing but comfort, I nodded off to sleep.

When I woke up, the birds were chirping, the sun was shining, and I felt serene—as if all of the years prior were one long and terrible nightmare.

A great sigh of relief, something that felt like it had been buried inside for an awfully long time, flowed out of me, and I felt the lightest, the freest I had ever felt in an awfully long time.

It was all over. All of the spirits were gone, even the one from New Jersey. I breathed in deeply, feeling a smile slowly spread across my face.

My new journey was very challenging at times.

For instance, I should have never believed that David would hold onto my things. My pictures, clothing and undergarments, furniture, pots and pans, and everything else in that small apartment. No matter how many calls I placed, he wouldn't pick up. Finally, I asked Tony to call, and David told him that he didn't have anything that belonged to me and to never call him again.

I was devastated.

I could have lived with any other loss, but our family's picture album was the lowest blow David dealt me. I was sure it was punishment for every time I did the opposite of what he wanted. Over time, I began to view the entire thing as if it was a fire or a natural disaster. No one recovers their pictures in those scenarios.

Still, I was tormented by this particular loss. That album had meant *everything* to me. So much, in fact, that one night I snuck into the kitchen after Tony and Kendall were in their room for the evening. Ignoring the gnawing feeling that began to rise from my stomach to my throat, I picked up the phone. I dialed the familiar number, thinking that I could convince David to return my things. Of course, there was no reason that he'd pick up. For the numerous times I'd called, he'd never answered me. But maybe this time would be different?

Hoping against hope, I heard the phone ring and ring...and the connection was made. "Hello, Keeya." David's voice sounded unsurprised, as if he had been waiting for this moment to happen. As if he knew it would happen.

Caught off guard that he had answered, I pushed back the unease I felt at his reception and spoke my reason for calling. "David," I stated firmly, "I don't want anything else except to make arrangements for my things. I know you still have them. I—"

"I believed in you!" He suddenly exclaimed, his voice strangely amplified. It had altered and now sounded inhuman. As if his voice was coming from another world. It couldn't be *Hell*, could it...?!

At his words, the hairs on the back of my neck rose immediately, and I stiffened as a cold fear zipped up my spine. Panicking, I dropped the phone, which clattered noisily on the counter. Knowing this had been a mistake, I managed to pick the receiver back up and jam it on the cradle, severing the connection.

For a moment, I just stood there, aware of the sudden silence, of my heart thudding wildly against my ribcage. I exhaled a shaky breath.

When I had ended our connection, I knew that things were finally over between us. No one had to tell me to cut my losses and move on. I heard the message loud and clear!

As alarming as this brief encounter was, I had needed the reminder that my past had nothing valuable enough in it to go back and try to salvage. My past was officially an unnatural disaster, and I was lucky to have my life. Even as I shook off the lingering strands of fear and went back to bed, I knew things would be better from now on. Needless to say, I was grateful to wake up to sunshine the next morning. And things did begin to look up—in a wonderfully *normal* way.

I eventually landed a job working at Wendy's, which was a humbling experience. It was an older facility, but the manager had a great relationship with his employees. Again, I didn't fit in as the new girl. The store was located in an economically challenged area. I got cussed out at the drive-thru on a regular basis. Not that I wasn't used to that in the clubs that I had worked at, but back then I made enough money to overlook most of it. I think I got cussed out the most at the Golden Lady in the Bronx and I'd done my fair share of returning the insults. My response at Wendy's was different, though. When I got cussed at, I followed up with an apology. I knew that my heart was changing. I really cared about my job, so I wanted to do my best to turn the other cheek.

Every pay day was sobering. The check was so small that I couldn't see how I was going to save up for my own place. I couldn't live on $89 a week—nobody could. I began to look for new opportunities. I searched through the classified job ads, circling the ones I was interested in, making calls, and setting up interviews.

Every week, I hung on to the encouraging sermons that the pastor preached. He always encouraged the congregation to "Get ready! Get ready, G-g-g-g-et R-e-a-d-y!" For me, his words spurred me to always do my best. I loved the hope that I now had with my new surroundings. I practically had no social life apart from church on Sunday mornings and Wednesday nights. And often, as we would pull into the parking lot, I would look at the university campus that stood right behind the church and dream of being a student there. Maybe, even at twenty-three, I could still live on the campus?

I wanted a better life, a life full of normalcy where I went to church and work and school while I pursued a degree. Maybe this was possible for me now? I held tightly to that belief—that life was worth living because I could have a future that was wonderfully normal.

I finally found a job working for ATC Communications Group. It was a very interesting place where a lot of immigrants and people from the wrong side of the tracks worked. I was definitely from the wrong side of the tracks, but I hid it well enough. From the ways I spoke and dressed, I appeared to be in management, or at least that's what people in the breakroom would say. I always received compliments on how I carried myself. This was encouraging to me because I felt so aware of my internal struggles. I realized that if I just worked hard and treated people well, I could live a normal life. No one would ever have to know my dirty secrets and the past life that I was so ashamed of.

I began to meet ladies who loved to talk about God and church; in fact, I gravitated toward them. And in turn, I longed to tell the women I met at work, who bragged about their lives of clubbing and heavy drinking and escapades with men, that it wasn't worth it in the long run. I often shied away from those conversations because I was afraid to reveal just how I knew the lifestyle they were praising would turn out. Besides, I had work to do.

I had an immense need to figure out how I would come to terms with my past but still not let the cat out of the bag. I was afraid of being judged. I was even more terrified of possibly losing a friend if they knew who I was. Maybe they wouldn't be able to handle it? I would at times test people who were getting close with a piece of a story, just to see their reaction. If they couldn't handle the little things, then I knew just how mild our connection would be.

This fear drove me to learn more about God. I knew that He was accepting of me and desired to change me. It was so comforting for me to read in the Bible about women who lived as prostitutes, and Jesus would tell them things like, "Go and sin no more," or "Your sins are forgiven." Jesus was so full of compassion that people followed Him, knowing they would be healed. I desperately needed this healing, and with each sermon I absorbed, I felt better about this new relationship with God. When Bishop Jakes would preach, it was just as if he knew me personally. I was amazed at how he could take the same scriptures I was reading and make real-life connections in such powerful ways.

I loved Bishop Jakes, but not because of his celebrity status. It was obvious that he wasn't the average pastor, but that didn't distract me very much. I was just happy to hear him declare life over me and teach me how to live and to get past my past. He spoke to all of us like we were his kids, and his voice was one of the strongest voices of wisdom in my life. I even felt like the relationship that I didn't have with Daddy would be okay if I embraced what this spiritual father was teaching.

And Lady Jakes was equally impactful. She carried herself so gracefully, so confident in her position and in the God who raised her up. She spoke and prayed so fervently, I could feel her love from a distance. Her warmth and her soothing words would grip me as if she was embracing and rubbing my sorrows away. Her powerful and penetrating prayers helped me regain my dignity. Sometimes, I would go to the altar for prayer and she would hug me. She had no clue how that was the acceptance I needed for the week.

I studied them and the ways they related to each other as husband and wife, always so honoring and loving. Their relationship gave me something to hope for, to strive for. They mirrored what I'd never seen: a strong black family who was successful because they loved God and lived for Him publicly. I wished that I could hug them both and tell them just how much their words brought healing and direction to my life.

It was as if God was giving me everything I had missed growing up.

Church became my counseling sessions where I could dig deep and not feel as if I was being treated for being crazy. My diagnosis became more about sin that led me to my savior and less about the chemicals and side effects that kept me off balance. Although those things were a very real part of my life, I responded better to them because of the help that my new environment provided. I found a community that was just as broken as I was, all in different ways—and we were each receiving the healing we needed. In such wonderful ways, God was using this church to breathe life back into my shell-shocked soul.

There was so much help at church for those wanting to gain life skills, too. For example, I faithfully attended a class to learn the skills needed to pass my GED. I didn't feel ashamed in coming because everyone in that class was just like me, some even much older than I was. The environment was so wonderful. I began to actually believe that I could one day be smart enough to fit in with the rest of the world. It was a start. A new beginning. I continued to heed the words of my spiritual father—Get ready, get ready, get, get, get, get ready!!

Also, I didn't just heal spiritually, but physically and emotionally as well. As time passed, surrounded by such love, joy, and compassion, I cannot describe the feeling of normal in any way other than that I physically felt I didn't need the medicine anymore. After the night of the hellish encounter in my brother's living room, everything had begun to change, including my dependence on the meds. Although I still took them for a few months, I eventually switched to a holistic approach of natural medicine and exercise. I felt like I had completely snapped out of my depressed state of mind.

When Sunday came, I usually responded to the altar call, which is an invitation to either accept Jesus Christ into your heart for the first time or to rededicate your life to Him. When I was seven, I had accepted Jesus into my heart already, so I opted to rededicate my life as many times as it took for me to believe it. This went on for months before Tony assured me that it only took one time and God did all of the work. But I wasn't sure he understood that *I* needed to make sure I was really severed from that life. My return home was like the prodigal son's in the Bible. The low ways I'd been accustomed to were nothing like this new safety of home. So, I continued every Sunday morning and Wednesday evening a few more times, and I even repeated the prayer and response to the altar call while I watched Trinity Broadcasting Network at home. I wanted God to know that I was serious. I never wanted to do the things that led up to my diagnosis ever again.

I was on the road to recovery, but I was not the only one aware of the newness in my life: my nervous breakdown brought Mommy, Tony, and me all closer together. Eventually, Mommy left Atlanta to be near and help me adjust to my new life. And, because of their devotion to me, I decided to finally share with them how I'd really been managing my life.

It was such a relief to *finally* tell them, the burden of so many secrets for so long *finally* being lifted from my shoulders.

The most beautiful part was that, through the painful revelations and countless conversations, they forgave and loved me through it all. I never once felt rejected by them, only loved. Trust me, I tested them in certain conversations to see if they, like others, were going to give up on me. But they never did.

What they *did* do is challenge me to continue serving God and to take the limits off my thinking. Yet while the external conversations were positive, internally I still battled with my low self-esteem. There was no number of sermons I could listen to that would reverse the work that only I was capable of reversing. And that would take time. As I learned through my life skills class, if you have the right information and don't apply it, it's of little value to you. You will be motivated, but without the correct tools, such motivation will be short-lived and achieve empty results. To have lasting success, I had to learn how to uproot my well-worn patterns of self-sabotage. That was a skill that would take time and patience. For the moment, I chose to accept the healing at the stage I was in, and that was good enough for me.

God used my family and their constant love to wipe layers of fear away from years of being away from Him. I had read a verse that reminded me of the significance of being with God. Those words rang so true in my life. The writer states in Psalm 84:10, "Better is one day in Your courts than a thousand elsewhere; I would rather be a doorkeeper in the house of my God than dwell in the tents of the wicked."

I decided from reading that verse that I would serve the God of my youth more boldly than I had served the god of elsewhere. I didn't need to be recognized. In fact, I was happier behind the scenes. I looked for opportunities to volunteer in ways that meant something to me. I volunteered in the women's ministry, in the youth department, and at conferences. Any place where I could serve people and put a smile on someone's face, doing the work of the Master the right way—that's where I wanted to be!

Eventually, I made enough money to move out of my brother's house into an apartment. I bought my second car, which wasn't the sleek, cream Infinity with the two-toned sand-and-black leather interior that I drove from club to club, but a cute, little burgundy Nissan with grey fabric seats that I bought with honest, hard-earned cash that I saved through my job at the ATC center. My roommate, who was the supervisor at the call center, and her friends drove me to the lot to pick out the new-to-me car. I was so proud of my accomplishment. I didn't need a sugar daddy to co-sign, I didn't have to expose myself to get ahead. I had honest, wholesome friendships that were developing and a new life to live in the city I had vowed never to return to.
I guess God had other plans.

I was reunited with two out of three family members. Daddy was no longer physically in the picture, although I did manage to speak with him briefly. I hadn't grown to forgive him totally yet; my heart was still healing. I learned not to push myself into areas that my heart was unable to handle. I was content with the love being shown to me by Mommy, Tony, and Kendall. If not for them, I don't know where or how I would have recovered. The road to full recovery was still ahead of me, and with my new-found faith, I would surely be just fine. I felt a sense of purpose as I soaked up the message of Christ from week to week. I couldn't get enough of Jesus being in and around me.

This way of life was a far cry from what I experienced just

months ago. Instead of nights frequenting a nice hotel with a football player, dancing for the average Joe, or visiting the Hotel Nikko for an after party, I was now working a regular job, surrounding myself with warm, godly people, and embracing the new life God had for me one day at a time.

With each day, I am getting stronger, more confident, and more excited about what God is doing in my life. And I can't wait to see what new plans He has in store for me!

The End